The
Sabbath

The Sabbath

by

Samuel H. Dresner

THE BURNING BUSH PRESS
NEW YORK

FOREWORD

Over a half-century ago, the eminent Jewish philosopher Hermann Cohen wrote the following lines: "Had Judaism brought into the world only the Sabbath, it would thereby have proved itself to be a producer of joy and a promoter of peace for mankind. The Sabbath was the first step on the road which led to the abrogation of slavery."

In the pages which follow, Rabbi Samuel H. Dresner has set for himself the task of depicting this joy of the Sabbath and the part that "the seventh day" can play in the liberation of Man from modern-day bondage. Drawing upon a wide variety of sources — ancient and modern, Jewish and general — the author evokes an appreciation of the Sabbath in its role as creator of peace between man and nature, man and society, and man and himself.

Rabbi Dresner provides the reader with an insightful analysis of the concept of *Shabbat* and its influence over the many centuries of Jewish history. This in turn is accompanied by a blueprint for Sabbath observance in our time. Rather than set down an "all-or-nothing" approach, he offers a reliable guide in the form of a ladder of Jewish observance. In combining this historical overview with a practical guide to Jewish living, Rabbi Dresner has created a valuable complement to his well-known essay *The Jewish Dietary Laws: Their Meaning for Our Time.*

The National Academy is pleased to sponsor *The Sabbath,* as one in its publication series dealing with the fundamentals of Jewish life. May it lead not only to an increased appreciation of the basic concept but also to deeper commitment to the *mitzvah* of *shemirat Shabbat.*

MARVIN S. WIENER, *Director*
National Academy for Adult Jewish Studies
of the United Synagogue of America

CONTENTS

I

The Struggle for Existence

"The struggle for existence."

"The survival of the fittest."

These striking phrases were first associated with Charles Darwin and his theory of evolution. So clearly descriptive of all of reality did they seem, however, that it was not long before thinkers and writers had seized upon them and were widely employing them not only in scientific journals to describe conditions of plant and animal life, but in novels, essays and works of philosophy to depict the very situation of man. What had begun as a tentative biological theory, debated and discussed by scientists, ended as a total philosophy of life which was accepted enthusiastically as the truth about mankind by a majority of the creative minds of our time.

"I believe life is a mess," wrote novelist Wolf Larsen. "It is like a yeast, a ferment, a thing that moves or may move for a minute, an hour, a year or a hundred years, but that in the end will cease to move. The big eat the little that they may continue to move, the strong eat the weak that they may retain their strength. The lucky eat the most and move the longest, that is all."

"Every man for himself — that was his maxim." So novelist Frank Norris described one of his heroes. "It might be damned selfish, but it was human nature; the weakest to the wall, the strongest to the front. . . . All life was but a struggle to keep from under those myriad spinning wheels that dashed so close behind. Those were the happiest who were farthest to the front. To lay behind was peril; to fall was to perish: to be ridden down, to be beaten to the dust, to be inexorably crushed and blotted out beneath that myriad of spinning wheels."

Beneath the apparent quiet and beauty of nature — the fragrance of the flowers, the flight of the bird, the glow of the sunset — there is a seething ferment of intrepid and uninterrupted warfare which knows neither clemency nor compromise and recognizes neither mercy nor compassion. It is a battle unending between all the manifold inhabitants of the world of nature. Fish, birds, animals, plants — all are engaged in this titanic struggle for existence. The strongest survive; the weak are left behind. Man, too, is a part of nature and, therefore, a part of this struggle. True, he is somewhat farther along the ladder of evolution, but in essence his fate is no different from that of the plants or animals in the world about him. Indeed, the social context of his so-called sophisticated existence is understood only by applying to it the same striking phrases, "struggle for existence" and "survival of the fittest."

The quotations from Wolf Larsen and Frank Norris are representative of many contemporary writers whose task is to describe the life of man as they see it. The writer looks our world squarely in the face with keen, analytical eyes. And he is sick at what he sees. Violence. Lust. Avarice. Anarchy. The end of all restraint. Cities become jungles; men of reason are tyrannized; brutality replaces books — a back-to-nature movement that has given free reign to all the terrors of the beast within. That is why today's writer uses the words and ideas of Darwin. That is why he writes of man as an animal. That is why he offers little hope. Defeat predominates over victory, competition over cooperation, jealousy over love, hatred over compassion, dissension over harmony. Not peace but war is the natural way of man's life.

Nor is such a description of man as animal limited to our own age; it can be found, no matter what the age or society, in French, German, Latin, and Greek literature of the past as well as in American literature of the present. Throughout history there resounds the mournful dirge of Thomas Hobbes: "The life of man is solitary, poor, nasty, brutish and short," for his condition is "a condition of war of everyone against everyone." Man as a belligerent beast is a major theme of world literature for a very simple reason: it contains an element of undeniable truth. Much of man's life is a constant warfare with conflicts on several levels: man is at war with nature, with society and with himself.

First of all, man is at war with *nature*.

He must contend constantly with the heat of the sun, the might of the ocean, the assault of deadly germs. He must build dikes to keep out the pounding waves, plant trees to fight soil erosion, invent drugs to prevent disease, erect houses to protect himself from the rigors of weather. His sprawling cities are magnificent achievements in the endless task of subduing nature and proving that he is master of the elements. But let him relax his vigil for a moment, forget about a small hole in the dike, fail to check the source of some disease, err ever

so slightly in the construction of his house, act care-
lessly in his city planning — and the grinding forces of
nature will be upon him, seeking to destroy all that he
has built and to swallow up all that he has labored for.

Secondly, man is at war with *society*.

If there is conflict between man and nature, and if
only the fittest survive, what can we say of the relation
between man and society, that is, between man and
his fellow man? Does not the struggle for material gain
constitute a struggle for existence just as ruthless, just
as endless, just as bitter as that between man and nature?
Every office is a battleground and each business venture
an occasion for warfare. Between nine and five the clash
of arms resounds. Who will receive the next order? Who
will be granted the next raise? Which competitor will
win the next bid? Who will succeed and who will fail?
These issues agitate and arouse the spirit of competition
and conflict. "Ambition," "profit motive," "success," are
hardly words conducive to peaceful living. They are no
more than streamlined, air-conditioned versions of a
savage and primitive battle cry. Between man and man,
too, there is warfare — a constant, never-ending battle.

Thirdly, man is at war with *himself*.

What is true of the struggles between man and nature,
and man and society, is likewise true of the struggle between man and himself. He is at war not only with the
world about him, but also with the world within him,
contending not merely with outer forces but with inner
forces as well. There is the constant clash between what
he should be and what he wants to be, between higher
interests and self-interest, between spirit and flesh, soul
and body, good and evil, God's will and man's own. This,

too, is a never-ending battle — a battle not easily discernible to the eye, an inner battle, but a battle nonetheless — just as fierce, just as cruel, just as harmful as the one he fights with nature or with his fellow man.

On all three levels then — with nature, with society and with one's self — life seems to be one great struggle for existence.

Is this the total meaning of life?

How can we find a way to end this warfare?

How can we find a road that will lead to peace?

II

The Sabbath: An Answer

Judaism makes a bold claim. It claims that it possesses an answer — a way to end man's warfare, a road that will lead to peace, a means of bringing about a cessation of hostilities on all three levels of conflict. It is an answer which, at first, seems strange, out of place, even absurd. It is no wonder, then, that in ancient times pagan peoples laughed at the Israelites and called them "lazy" because they ceased to work one day in seven, or that in modern times pagans among our own people — among Jews themselves — have failed to understand it, forgetting its glory and power, discarding it as a relic of the past in the hasty process of Americanization (unaware of the fact that it is through our faith that we are defined as Americans and contribute to our country). It is an answer which has escaped the eye even of those who diligently search for the solution to a problem which devastates so much of human life and spirit.

It is the Sabbath!

The Sabbath holds within its bounds one of the surest means of finding peace in the war-torn realm of the soul. It is one of the basic institutions of humanity — an idea with infinite potentiality, infinite power, infinite hope, perhaps, as some claim, the single most significant contribution of Judaism to world culture. Through the Sabbath, Judaism has succeeded in turning its greatest teachings into a day. Out of a remote world of profound thoughts, grand dreams and fond hopes — all of which seem so distant, so intangible and so unrealizable — the Sabbath has forged a living reality which can be seen and tasted and felt at least once a week. "The Sabbath is the hub of the Jew's universe," wrote Israel Zangwill; "to protract it is a virtue; to love it a liberal education." Among the Ten Commandments only one observance, one holiday, is mentioned — not Passover or the Day of Atonement, but the Sabbath: "Remember the Sabbath day, to keep it holy" (Exodus 20:8). It is the supreme symbol of Judaism, a recurring sign and reminder of creation and redemption.

Even the Festivals cannot compare to the Sabbath. The Festivals, said Rabbi Moshe of Kobrin, are like a poor man who is visited by a great king. Though the honor of the visit brings him joy, he is still aware of his own poverty. On the Sabbath, however, the pauper is invited into the king's palace where all awareness of his humble station vanishes.

The Rabbi of Ger gave a different reason. He said that the Festivals are bound by time, while the Sabbath is an aspect of eternity. Thus the Festivals come at fixed seasons of the year — the spring, the early harvest and the late harvest — and bring blessings to each season. But the Sabbath, because it partakes of the timeless, is the source of all blessings. It is, as Abraham Heschel has said, "eternity uttering a day."*

The Sabbath has taught us how to sanctify time and bring a dimension of holiness into the profane rhythm of life; how to unite a way of thinking with a way of living and join body and soul, heart and mind to the service of God; how to be worthy of having been created in His image and touch the hem of the world-to-come in this world; how to find a foretaste of heaven on earth and sense the eternal within the temporal. If Israel had done nothing more than give the Sabbath to mankind, it would deserve to be called "the chosen people."

But glorious though the Sabbath may be in theory and nostalgic though it may be in memory, in actual practice today it has all but been forfeited. Only scattered diehards still continue to maintain it in its dignity and grandeur. More and more it is defiled by the indifference of the majority and the ignorance of the mob who rumble over the sanctity of the day with neither understanding nor concern. The tendency of the Jew to attempt to conform to the prevailing pattern of the Gentile majority is powerful.

Most Jews in our time have never experienced an authentic Jewish Sabbath; what some of them did encounter in their youth was a version so emasculated and

---

* I am indebted to Dr. Heschel's profound study, *The Sabbath: Its Meaning for Modern Man,* for the basic concept out of which this book has developed.

vulgarized that it retained little of the original splendor.
It is only natural, therefore, for one to wonder just
what this seemingly dark day of "don'ts," this apparent
twenty-four-hour "denial of joy and freedom," has to do
with the all-embracing human problem of conflict. What
can a few old-fashioned customs and ceremonies, the
narrow folkways of a small people, have to do with any
universal concern of mankind?

To understand the nature of the Sabbath and the
manner in which the Jewish people have observed it
in their homes and in their lives, we must turn to the
meaning of two words, *Kallah* ("Bride"), and *Malkah*
("Queen"), by which terms the Sabbath has been known.

Kallah

Let us deal first with the term *Kallah,* or "Bride."

The Sabbath is often referred to in Jewish literature
as the Sabbath Bride, *Shabbat HaKallah.* Why? How
can a day become a person? This strange transformation
is precisely what happened in the course of the centuries
through which Israel's observance of the Seventh Day
grew and deepened and overflowed its former bounds.
The Sabbath came to be considered not simply a day
like any other day — abstract, opaque, comprised of so
many hours and minutes and seconds — but it took on
the characteristics of a living person whose presence
one became aware of and whom one looked upon with
affection and yearning. So much richness and meaning
did the day acquire in the course of the centuries that
it was treated not as a day at all, but as a wondrous and
gracious personality who poured forth an endless stream
of love and peace which was received and returned in

joy by all those who awaited her coming. According to the Talmud, God gave each day a mate. Thus Sunday had Monday, Tuesday had Wednesday, Thursday had Friday. Only the Sabbath day was alone. So God gave it to the people of Israel as its mate, as its bride.

Why is the Sabbath called a "bride"? What does the term symbolize? The symbol of a bride is love, devotion and joy — an inward feeling. It is this peculiar inward feeling of the Jew which characterizes the Sabbath day. To him the Sabbath is a bride. Just as one prepares for a bride with the utmost care and meticulous detail, so the Sabbath is preceded by careful preparation. Just as one yearns for the arrival of a bride, so is the Sabbath met and welcomed. Just as the presence of the bride elicits tender concern, so does the Sabbath evoke love and devotion. Just as the departure of a bride occasions sadness, so is the departure of the Sabbath in darkness and regret. In all ways she is *Shabbat HaKallah*, the Sabbath Bride.

What is the difference between the Christian Sunday and the Jewish Sabbath? One way to distinguish them is to ask yourself whether Sunday, now or in the past, could be transformed into a person, a bride? Sunday is followed by Monday, Tuesday, and so forth, each day having a special name and standing by itself. But to Jews only the seventh day — the Sabbath — has a name, the others but a number. Thus: the "first day," the "second day," or the "third day," in accordance with how near or far they are to the "seventh day." Sunday is a day of commencement, the beginning of a week of toil. The Sabbath is a day of completion, the end of a week of yearning. Sunday arrives at midnight when the world sleeps; it is received passively, automatically. But Jews must "make" Sabbath; they must prepare for it, for the bride will not show her face unless she is invited and loved.

According to the Talmud, the world was created only for the Sabbath Bride. " 'And on the seventh day God finished His work which He had made' (Genesis 2:2). Genibah and the Sages discussed the passage. Genibah explained it thus: It may be compared to a king who made a bridal chamber, which he plastered, painted and adorned. What did the chamber lack? The bride. Like-wise, what did the world still lack after six days of crea-tion? The Sabbath." [1]

> The Sabbath is a bride, and its celebration is like a wedding. . . .
>
> "There is a hint of this in the Sabbath prayers. In the Friday evening service we say *Thou hast sanctified the seventh day*, referring to the marriage of the bride to the groom (sanctification is the Hebrew word for marriage). In the morning prayer we say *Moses rejoiced in the gift* [of the Sabbath] bestowed upon him which corresponds to the groom's rejoicing with the bride. In the additional prayer we make mention of *the two lambs, the fine flour for a meal offering mingled with oil and the drink thereof*, referring to the meat, the bread, the wine and the oil used in the wedding banquet. [In the last hour of the day we say] *Thou art One*, to parallel the consummation of the marriage by which the bride and groom are united." [2]

A beautiful song was composed to welcome the Sab-bath Bride — *L'khah Dodi:*

> Bridegroom, come to meet the bride.
> Let us welcome the presence of the Sabbath.

The overflowing love of the people of Israel for their Bride-Sabbath led them over the centuries to set this poem to more melodies than any other prayer we possess. To the mystics of sixteenth-century Safed, where this poem was written, the synagogue was not grand enough to receive the Sabbath: its walls were too limiting, its presence too confining. So they would go out into the open fields, dressed in white, the color of the wedding garment, and there chant psalms and sing *L'khah Dodi,* accompanying the Sabbath Bride into their synagogues. Still today, when the last verse of the prayer is sung:

> Come in peace, and come in joy,
> Thou who art thy bridegroom's pride;
> Come, O bride, and shed thy grace
> O'er the faithful chosen race;
> Come, O bride! Come, O bride!

the congregation turns from the Ark, faces the entrance and bows to the Bride who is about to enter.

The Bride comes not only into the synagogue, but into the home and into the heart as well, bringing love and joy and song. A new tenderness is nurtured between mother and father, a new devotion between parents and children; and throughout the house a spirit of radiant joy permeates. No sadness is permitted on the Sabbath. Even the seven days of *shivah,* the mourning period, are interrupted for the Sabbath. The famous story from the Talmud of how Beruriah, the wife of Rabbi Meir, delayed telling her husband the terrible news of the death of their two sons until the Sabbath had passed and night had fallen, became a living example in countless Jewish homes through the ages, that one must take every precaution to preserve the sweet peace and joy of the day. Jews have always explained the special mood of exaltation they felt on the Sabbath, the inner tranquility and outer calm, the light that was said to shine from their faces, by claiming that with the arrival of each Seventh Day, God gives them an added soul, a *neshamah yeterah*. That is why we inhale from the spice box during the *Havdalah* ceremony when the Sabbath is ushered out on Saturday night: to revive us at the departure of the *neshamah yeterah*.

Rabbi Solomon of Radomsk once arrived in a certain town, where, he was told, lived an old woman who had known the famous Rabbi Elimelech. She was too old to go out, so he went to see her and asked her to tell him what she knew about the great Master.

— I do not know what went on in his room, because I worked as one of the maids in the kitchen of his house. Only one thing I can tell you. During the week the maids would often quarrel with one another, as is common. But, week after week, on Friday when the Sabbath was about to arrive, the spirit in the kitchen was like the spirit on the eve of the Day of Atonement. Everybody would be overcome with an urge to ask forgiveness of each other. We were all seized by a feeling of affection and inner peace.[3]

Malkah

But important as is the idea of *Kallah* for understanding the meaning of the Sabbath, testifying, as it does, to the presence of the Sabbath Bride who brings love and joy and inner peace, it alone is not adequate. It is only part of the meaning. There is also the term *Malkah* or "Queen," for the Seventh Day is also referred to as *Shabbat HaMalkah,* the "Sabbath Queen."

Why is the Sabbath called a Queen? What does the term symbolize?

If *Kallah,* or Bride, is the symbol of love, *Malkah,* or Queen, is the symbol of law; if *Kallah* evokes devotion, *Malkah* demands obedience; if *Kallah* stands for feeling, *Malkah* represents observance. Inwardness, important though it may be, is not enough. There must likewise be an outward form, a pattern of conduct, a definite way.

Indeed, one can never truly know the inward feeling of the Sabbath without the outward form. The Sabbath is not a theory to be contemplated, a concept to be debated or an idea to be toyed with. It is a day, a day filled with hours and minutes and seconds, all of which are hallowed by the wonderful pattern of living which the nobility of the human spirit has fashioned over the course of the centuries. One cannot shift the Sabbath to a different day each week. There is no "Sabbath on Tuesday." There is no "essence" of the Sabbath. There is only the joy of experiencing the Sabbath day itself: the release from work, the setting aside of all money, the blessing of the children, the kindling of the lights, the study of the Torah portion, the worship in the synagogue, the time spent with the family. Just as there can be no music without an instrument, no song without a voice, no soul without a body, so there can be no Sabbath spirit without Sabbath observance. This, perhaps, is the lesson which the following Talmudic story teaches.

The Roman Emperor Hadrian asked Rabbi Joshua ben Hananiah, "Why is it that Sabbath foods have such a fragrant scent?"

Rabbi Joshua answered, "We put in a certain spice called Sabbath."

The Emperor said, "Please give me some of that spice."
Rabbi Joshua answered, "It can be tasted only by those
who keep the Sabbath."

The Sabbath cannot be observed haphazardly, subject to the whims of each individual, as a day to be spent
at the golf club or before the television set, or time to
be used washing the car or mowing the lawn. The "week-
end," with its parties, liquor, noonday sleeping and un-
washed, unshaven faces, its high incidence of crime and
auto accidents, is more a denial of than a substitute for
the Sabbath.

The pattern of Sabbath observance aims at achieving
the goals of the Sabbath: love, joy and rest. It tells us
how to welcome the Sabbath, with what words and at
what times of the day; how to say farewell to the Sabbath,
with what words and at what time of the day. It prescribes fixed prayers, attendance at the synagogue, read-
ing of the Torah, a period of study, the lighting of
candles, the chanting of *Kiddush,* the singing of *zemirot.*
It prescribes the cessation of work and a separation from
all those affairs of the world which cause strife, anguish
and conflict, a removing of oneself from the trivial and
the vulgar, the unseemly and the banal, so that we can
once again be at home with Him Who ever seeks to enter
our lives. All of those observances form a pattern of behavior which complements, protects and engenders the
inward feeling already mentioned. And this pattern of
behavior is symbolic of *Shabbat HaMalkah,* the Sabbath
Queen, who reigns over the Jewish home in majestic
sovereignty, imposing her will, enjoining her rule, es-
tablishing her command from one generation to the next

through the authority of the hallowed *halakhah* (the path of the law), so that the way of Sabbath observance remains, for the most part, a constant way from age to age.

When a Queen is in the palace, everything must be just so. The tables and chairs are not askew; the rugs are newly cleaned; the floors are polished; and a mood of subservience to her majesty pervades the rooms. So it is with *Shabbat HaMalkah*. Her presence, too, demands that all be in order. But this order has a special purpose: to guarantee the mood of inner peace. She does this by decreeing that all work cease — no cooking, no washing, no shopping, no business to be transacted. That one may not be so tempted, even the instruments for work — pencils, tools, money, etc. — may not be touched. But this means that everything must be in readiness before the Sabbath begins, that no one need worry about buying a bottle of milk or sewing on a button or paying a bill or seeing a customer. Careful planning is required. The Seventh Day does not come pre-packaged. One flick of a magic switch will not turn it on. We must "make" *Shabbat*. Thus, even before the Sabbath arrives, the reign of the Queen is anticipated in preparations during the days before. The husband schedules his week so that he can leave early for home on Friday. The wife and children give priority to the Sabbath in planning their activities. By Friday afternoon, all final provisions are made. All *muktseh** is stored away. The washing, cooking, cleaning, dressing, and shaving have been completed.

---

* That which is not handled on the Sabbath because it may lead to a violation of the Sabbath, *e.g.*, a match or pencil.

And when at last the wife kindles the Sabbath candles,
it is not an arbitrary gesture acted out of impulse, but
rather a joyous yet solemn symbol that all stands in readiness. Chaos and care have been banished. The demands
of the Queen have been met. She is about to be received.

To those who are strange to Jewish law, it may seem
rigid, imposing, overwhelming. But when we begin to
make our way slowly along its well-worn paths, perceiv-
ing its wisdom and understanding its purpose, we learn
to appreciate it as one of the few roads that can lead man
safely through the wilderness of life. Franz Rosenzweig,
the famous *ba'al teshuvah* of pre-war Germany, describes
this journey in one of his letters. "Originally," he writes,
"I made it my principle to refrain from all business cor-
respondence on the Sabbath, but saw no harm in writing
letters to friends. Nor did I give up this way of keeping
the Sabbath until once when Henry Rothschild and I
were discussing some matter concerning the Lehrhaus
[the Jewish Adult School Rosenzweig founded], he tried
to make me jot down notes since — so he said — I did
not mind writing on the Sabbath. That experience,
which taught me how unfeasible it is to draw such fine
distinctions unless everyone else draws them too, finally
drove me to accept the traditional practice of not writing at all on the Sabbath, though to come to this decision
was not easy for me." [4]

He who wants to enter the holiness of the day must
first lay down the profanity of clattering commerce, of
being yoked to toil. He must go away from the screech of
dissonant days, from the nervousness and fury of acquisi-
tiveness and the betrayal in embezzling his own life. He
must say farewell to manual work and learn to under-

stand that the world has already been created and will survive without the help of man. Six days a week we wrestle with the world, wringing profit from the earth; on the Sabbath we especially care for the seed of eternity planted in the soul. The world has our hands, but our souls belong to Someone Else. Six days a week we seek to dominate the world, on the seventh day we try to dominate the self. . . . For all the idealization, there is no danger of the idea of the Sabbath becoming a fairy-tale. With all the romantic idealization, the Sabbath remains a concrete fact, a legal institution and a social order. There is no danger of its becoming a disembodied spirit, for the spirit of the Sabbath must always be in accord with actual deeds, with definite actions and abstentions. The real and the spiritual are one, like body and soul in a living man. It is for the law to clear the path; it is for the soul to sense the spirit.[5]

A man's mood, be it ever so ennobling, ever so profound, ever so praiseworthy, is frail, transient, open to change and transmutation. The Queen comes to prevent such change, to guarantee the mood, to lend stability and permanence to what might otherwise fly away. The *Kallah* — that symbol of inward feeling — is not enough; she needs the *Malkah* — that symbol of outward form — to give her strength and permanence.

Thus the Sabbath must be both Bride *and* Queen. One without the other is weak, unstable, untrue to the Jewish spirit which combines both *halakhah* and *aggadah*, prose and poetry, law and love, inward devotion and outward form. The love of the *Kallah* without the law of the *Malkah* would quickly fall to pieces and disintegrate; it would have no substance, no reality, no pattern of expression, no protection, no guarantee of permanence. On the other hand, the law of the *Malkah* without the love of the *Kallah* would mean a harsh, officious, legalistic day, a time of gloom and restriction and rebellion. Lest we think that these are two separate decrees, the Rabbis remind us that "God spoke the words, 'Remember' and 'Keep,' as one command" (Shevuot 20a). They are two sides of the same injunction. Bride and Queen are but names for different guises of the identical person. One moment she appears in regal splendor, the next in radiant joy, as a precious gem radiates various colors according to the light which strikes it. Therefore the Sabbath commandment is mentioned twice in Scripture, once in Exodus (20:8), where it is written, "Remember the Sabbath day," that is, Remember it in your heart and soul with joy and love and inner peace; and once in Deuteronomy (5:12), where it is written "Keep the Sabbath day," that is, Keep its laws and statutes with devotion and loyalty and steadfastness. The Sabbath is both Bride and Queen, both remembering and keeping, both inward feeling and outward observance. It is, in miniature, the entire Jewish religion.

Menuhah

In addition to *Kallah* and *Malkah*, there is a third word which we must now consider, for it represents the goal which both Bride and Queen seek to achieve, the very purpose of the Sabbath. That word is *Menuhah*, usually translated "rest." The Bride and Queen both serve to bring *menuhah*, by which the Sabbath itself is known. Thus it is called *Shabbat Menuhah*, "a Sabbath of rest," or sometimes the phrase is reversed so as to read *Menuhat Shabbat*, "the rest of the Sabbath." In either case it is clear that the two are inextricably joined in meaning and usage.

The words: "On the *seventh* day God *finished* His work" (Genesis 2:2), seem to be a puzzle. Is it not said: "He *rested* on the *seventh* day"? "In *six* days the Lord made heaven and earth" (Exodus 20:11)? We would surely expect the Bible to tell us that on the sixth day God finished His work. Obviously, the ancient rabbis concluded, there was an act of creation on the seventh day. Just as heaven and earth were created in six days, *menuha* was created on the Sabbath. "After the six days of creation — what did the universe still lack? *Menuha*. Came the Sabbath, came *menuha*, and the universe was complete."

Menuha which we usually render with "rest" means here much more than withdrawal from labor and exertion, more than freedom from toil, strain or activity of any kind. *Menuha* is not a negative concept but something real and intrinsically positive. This must have been the view of the ancient rabbis if they believed that it took a special act of creation to bring it into being, that the universe would be incomplete without it. . . . To the biblical mind *menuha* is the same as happiness and stillness, as peace and harmony. The word with which Job described the state after life that he was longing for is derived from the same root as *menuha*. It is the state wherein man lies still, wherein the wicked cease from troubling and the weary are at rest. It is the state in which there is no strife and no fighting, no fear and no distrust. . . . "The Lord is my shepherd, I shall not want, He maketh me to lie down in green pastures; He leadeth me beside the still waters" (the waters of *menuhot*).[6]

To help us understand the meaning of *Menuhah* we must go to the Sabbath afternoon service and read the

prayer *Atah Ehad,* one of the most sublime in our entire
liturgy.

Thou art One and Thy name is One,
And who is like Thy people Israel, one nation on the
   earth?
A crown of glory and salvation,
A day of rest and holiness,
Thou hast given unto Thy people.
Abraham is glad, Isaac rejoices,
Jacob and his sons find rest thereon.
A rest of love freely given,
A rest of truth and sincerity,
A rest in peace and tranquility, in quietude and safety,
A perfect rest in which Thou findest favor.
Let Thy children perceive and know
That this their rest is from Thee,
And by their rest they hallow Thy name.

*"Thou art One and Thy name is One, and who is
like Thy people Israel, one nation on the earth?"* As God
is one in all the world and His name is one in all the
world, so Israel is one in all the earth. In Israel's *tefillin*
is written: "Hear, O Israel, the Lord our God, the Lord
is One." God too wears *tefillin.* In God's *tefillin* is written: "Thou art One and Thy name is One, and who is
like Thy people Israel, one nation on the earth?" (Be-
rakhot 6a). The one God whose name is one has chosen
for Himself from among all the peoples the one people,
Israel, and has given to her, as a sign of His unending
love, His most precious gift, the Sabbath, that she might
find *menuhah* in it, and that all might recognize her
greatness and know her sovereignty.

"*. . . a day of rest and holiness . . .*" The Sabbath is "a day of rest and holiness," that is, of *Menuhah* and *Kedushah*. *Kedushah* emanates from God Himself. When the prophet Isaiah was awestruck at the glory of God's presence in the Temple in Jerusalem (6:1-5), the word that rang in his ears, as if uttered by the angels, was *kadosh*. "*Kadosh, kadosh, kadosh* (holy, holy, holy) is the Lord of hosts." He is called the God of holiness, *Kedosh Yisrael*, the "Holy One of Israel," or, more simply, *HaKadosh Barukh Hu*, "the Holy One, blessed be He." Therefore, the day which He gives to Israel must be a day of *kedushah*. But that is not all it is. It is also a day of *menuhah*, of rest, of repose, of tranquility. It is a day of *kedushah* and *menuhah*. Indeed, it is a day of .*kedushah because* it is a day of *menuhah*. The *kedushah* of the day depends upon the *menuhah*. Holiness, in this case, is defined by rest: *kedushah* by *menuhah*.

We sanctify the Sabbath not only with words and gestures but by the very manner of our repose. The way in which we rest determines whether or not the Sabbath possesses holiness. For just as in the marketplace "the Holy One is made holy by righteousness," so on the Seventh Day is He sanctified by our inner tranquility.

"*Abraham is glad, Isaac rejoices, Jacob and his sons find* menuhah *thereon* (on the Sabbath)." Abraham and Isaac are glad, remarks one commentator, because Jacob and his children, the whole household of Israel, find *menuhah* on the Sabbath.

But what is this *menuhah* which we haltingly translate as "rest" — a special kind of rest which fits only the Sabbath? The prayer from the Sabbath *Minhah* service goes on to touch upon the various meanings which the word has.

It is *"a* menuhah *of love."* The Sabbath is no unpleasant yoke to which we are harnessed but a day we wait for and welcome with affection, as we would a bride. The spirit of the *Shabbat Kallah* must prevail.

"... *freely given* ..." Our love for the Sabbath is freely given, as for a bride, and is more than an obligation. Thus we anticipate it before sunset and remain with it after nightfall, adding to the holy from the profane out of the innermost yearning of our hearts.

"... *a* menuhah *of truth and sincerity* ..." The Sabbath permits of no duplicity; tongue and heart are joined; one says what one believes and one does what one says.

"... *a* menuhah *in peace and tranquility, in quietude and safety* ... " All that is broken during the week is mended on this day, brought together into a joyous whole (*shalom =* completeness), as if the *Shabbat Malkah* had sent out a decree, closing off all commerce, all labor, all disconcerting elements, all movements and actions which might disrupt the peace of the day, spreading over us the shelter of her rule, providing a pattern of observance in whose mysteries we find the quietude and safety the week denies. "The older I become and better understand its ways," wrote Franz Rosenzweig, "the more I appreciate the blessing that resides in its *menuhah*."

"... *a perfect* menuhah ..." If it is true and sincere, filled with love and freely given, a haven of security, a day of the Bride and Queen, then it is "perfect," a *menuhah* "in which Thou findest favor."

"Let Thy children perceive and know that this their menuhah *is from Thee, and by their* menuhah *they hallow Thy name."* The prayer concludes with a plea that

we never forget the two things about *menuhah* which makes the Sabbath.

We must never forget that its source is in heaven — "this their *menuhah* is from Thee." It is as if, after having recounted the glory, the joy and the peace which Sabbath *menuhah* brings, we are warned, lest, holding the great treasure in our domain, we take it for granted, demean it, and come to consider it our very own: Do not think that this day, which is more than a day — rather a sign between God and man — is your own possession, conceived, formed, and created by your finite, mortal mind. It is not only you who keep the Sabbath; the Lord Himself kept the first Sabbath. This *menuhah*, so dear to Israel, so necessary for all mankind, is not man's invention but God's creation. "Their *menuhah* comes from Thee."

The last sentence of the prayer bids us keep in mind that the *menuhah* which is the Sabbath has been given to Israel, and through it we have the power to hallow, that is, to bring *kedushah* to the Lord. "By their (Israel's) *menuhah* they hallow Thy name." The Sabbath comes from God but it was given to man. The Sabbath is God's creation but it is also His gift, His most precious gift, which He has handed over to Israel to love and to observe, that they might find *menuhah* in it and thus bring holiness to God. This too we must never forget. Especially this we must never forget.

Thus the children of Israel should "perceive and know" two things: the origin of Sabbath *menuhah* and its destiny; its source and its purpose: the glory of the One who gave it and the greatness of the one to whom it was given (both of whom are "one" or unique). We are humbled as the recipients, and strengthened at the wonder we have received; grateful that the Sabbath was given to us, and awed that by our observance of the Sabbath we can sanctify the Lord Himself. Israel is dependent upon God, for He created the Sabbath. God is dependent upon Israel, for unto us it has been given and through our keeping it He is hallowed. His *kedushah* depends upon Israel's *menuhah*. The way in which Israel keeps the Sabbath — the extent to which she is able to find *menuhah* on that day — not only determines her own fate but the fate of the Lord Himself.

The *Kallah* and the *Malkah* both strive to bring *menuhah*. It is, therefore, through an appreciation of these three — *Kallah, Malkah* and *menuhah* — that we come to understand the mystery of the Sabbath.

Experiencing the Sabbath

Words are weak, ideas fragmentary, their power fearfully limited. To fathom the grandeur of the Sabbath and perceive something of its splendor — how outward form and inward spirit blend into the miracle of a day — one must experience its existential reality and observe how it has been, and still is, being lived by faithful Jews throughout the world, who week after week taste something of its glory and its peace.

How well I remember when, as a college student, I first experienced a traditional Sabbath evening.

The head of the house returned from the synagogue with the children and, as they entered the door which opened into a room that glowed with Sabbath candles and Sabbath cleanliness, all began to sing *Shalom Aleikhem,* greeting the Sabbath angels who come to visit each

Jewish home Friday night and carry with them the rich blessing of Sabbath peace:

> Welcome, O ministering angels,
> Angels from on high,
> Who come from the King of kings,
> The Holy One, blessed be He.
>
> Enter in peace, angels of peace,
> Angels from on high,
> Who come from the King of kings,
> The Holy One, blessed be He.
>
> Bless me with peace, angels of peace,
> Angels from on high,
> Who come from the King of kings,
> The Holy One, blessed be He.
>
> Then go in peace, angels of peace,
> Angels from on high,
> Who come from the King of kings,
> The Holy One, blessed be He.

Then, seated at the table, the husband chanted *Eyshet Hayil*, that song of endearment from the thirty-first chapter of the Book of Proverbs with which Jewish husbands serenade their wives each Sabbath eve, renewing their love once again:

> A woman of valor who can find?
> Her price is far above rubies.
> The heart of her husband trusteth in her,
> And he shall have no lack of gain.
> She doeth him good and not evil,
> All the days of her life. . . .

She giveth food to her household,
And a portion for her maidens. . . .
She stretcheth out her hand to the poor,
Yea, she reacheth forth her hands to the needy. . . .
Strength and dignity are her clothing,
And she laugheth at the time to come.
She openeth her mouth with wisdom,
And the law of lovingkindness is on her tongue.
She looketh well to the ways of her household,
And eateth not the bread of idleness.
Her children rise up and call her blessed,
Her husband also, and he praiseth her:
"Many daughters have done worthily,
But thou excellest them all."
Grace is deceitful, and beauty is vain,
But a woman that revereth the Lord, she shall be
    praised.
Give her of the fruit of her hands,
And let her works praise her in the gates.

A hushed solemnity followed while each child, beginning with the eldest and ending with the youngest, hum-
bly bent his head to receive the eagerly awaited weekly
blessing from father and mother:

May God make thee as Ephraim and Manasseh.
May God make thee as Sarah, Rebekah, Rachel and
    Leah.
May the Lord bless thee and keep thee.
May the Lord cause His countenance to shine upon
    thee and be gracious unto thee.
May the Lord lift up His countenance towards thee
    and give thee peace.

Shining silver cups, brimful and sparkling with wine, were raised while the words of the *Kiddush* were chanted: "Blessed art Thou, O Lord our God, King of the universe, Who hast sanctified us by Thy commandments and hast taken pleasure in us, and in love and favor hast given us Thy holy Sabbath as an inheritance. . . ." The hands were washed, the blessing said over the two loaves of bread — a reminder of the double portion of manna which fell on Friday so that none should be gathered on the Sabbath — and the meal began.

But it was not just a meal; it was a sanctification of the profane, a means of exalting the common task of eating. Nor was it just a table; it was an altar: therefore the washing of the hands, therefore the salt, therefore the covering of the knife — a symbol of war, not tolerated upon the altar, the symbol of peace — during the Grace following the meal. Nor was it just a family sitting down to dinner, but rather Priests and Levites engaged in a sacred ritual, ministering in the holy temple of the home.

Between each course *zemirot* were sung, songs which speak of the beauty of the Sabbath and the observance of the Sabbath, and during each course the conversation drew from the endless well of Torah. One felt the meaning of the passage, "When three sit together and words of Torah are spoken, it is as if they had eaten at the Lord's table" (Avot 3:4).

When the meal was concluded, the family recited the Grace which included a special prayer for the day: "Be pleased, O Lord our God, to strengthen us by Thy commandments, and especially by the commandment of the Seventh Day, the great and holy Sabbath, since this day

is great and holy before Thee, that we may rest and repose thereon in love in accordance with the precept of
Thy will. In Thy favor, O Lord our God, grant us such
rest that there be no trouble, grief or lamenting on the
day of our rest." Then books were brought out and
given to each one for a period of study of the Torah portion of the week with Rashi's Commentary. By now
guests had arrived who joined in this Friday night study
period. Finally, while the candles were burning low
and the shadows were lengthening along the walls, all
joined in singing Hebrew songs until late in the evening.

In such a home one knows what it means to dwell
in the presence of the Sabbath Bride and the Sabbath
Queen. One tastes of the *menuhah* which is the Sabbath.

In a reverie I walked home under the starry heavens,
tears brimming in my eyes, my mind resting on the miracle of being a Jew.

III

Sabbath Peace

If what we have said about the meaning and grandeur
of the Sabbath is understood — that it is both Bride and
Queen, inner spirit and outer form — and if the atmosphere of *menuhah* is understood as being a harmony of
feeling and observance, then we are able to realize why
it is that the Sabbath can be the answer to the conflict
our fitful lives are involved in, to the struggle we are
engaged in with nature, with society, and with ourselves.
It spells an end to all conflict, a halt to all struggles; it

stands for peace in every aspect of life. Let us see how this is so in each of these three areas of strife: how the Sabbath brings peace between man and nature, between man and society, and between man and himself.

Peace Between Man and Nature

The Sabbath brings peace *between man and nature.* Regarding man's conflict with nature, Erich Fromm has pointed out that:

> The concept of work underlying the Biblical and the later Talmudic concept is not simply that of physical effort but can be defined thus: *Work is any interference by man, be it constructive or destructive, with the physical world. "Rest" is a state of peace between man and nature* [Italics supplied]. Man must leave nature untouched, not change it in any way, neither by building nor by destroying anything; even the smallest change made by man in the natural process is a violation of "rest." The Sabbath is the day of peace between man and nature; work is any kind of disturbance of the man-nature equilibrium. On the basis of this general definition, we can understand the Sabbath ritual. Indeed any heavy work like plowing or building is work in this as well as in our modern sense. But even lighting a match and pulling up a blade of grass, while not requiring effort, are symbols of human interference with the natural process, are a breach of the peace between man and nature.[7]

On the Sabbath we are at peace with nature. Six days a week we compete with the natural world — building, subduing, struggling to overcome lest we be overcome. Technology is our bible; the machine, our god; and gadgets, the holy vessels we revere. On the Seventh Day we withdraw, moving from creation to Creator, from machine and gadget to the quiet of our souls, from nature to the Lord of all nature, from conflict to *Shabbat Menuhah* — innermost rest and harmony. Nothing is created on the Sabbath; there is no sewing, no cooking, no building, no writing — nothing which can interfere with the sense of rest. One day a week we are at peace with nature.

Is man creature or creator? In his victory over the forces of nature, whose deepest secrets he unravels — turning great forests into farms and cities, drawing forth from the earth gold, silver and precious stones, harnessing powerful rivers to provide untold energy, learning to fly through the air like a bird and swim through the water like a fish, conquering dreaded diseases that were the scourge of society for centuries, building towers that pierce the clouds and trains to carry thousands underground, splitting the atom into incomprehensible power and discovering how to ascend even to the moon — it is to be expected that man would be tempted to consider himself the lord of all, the mastermind of the universe. It is so easy for him to think of himself not as creature but as creator, the all-knowing, all-seeing, all-dominating lord of nature. Infatuated with his marvelous talents, he may forget the real Creator, without whom all man's achievements are as nothing, all his gadgets dust, all his inventions instruments that can be turned into terrible weapons which can destroy, rather than improve the world. For the real purpose of life is not to conquer nature but to conquer the self; not to fashion a city out of a forest but to fashion a soul out of a human being; not to build bridges but to build human kindness; not

to learn to fly like a bird or swim like a fish but to walk
on the earth like a man, not to erect skyscrapers but to
establish mercy and justice, not to manufacture an in-
genious technical civilization but to be holy in the midst
of unholiness. The real tasks are to learn how to remain
civilized in the midst of insanity, how to retain a share
in man's dignity in the midst of the Dachaus and Buchen-
walds, how to keep the mark of Cain from obscuring the
image of the divine, how to fashion a home of love and
peace, how to create children obedient and reverent,
how to find the strength to perform the *mitzvot,* how to
bend our will to God's will.

There must be rest from work on the Sabbath [wrote
Samson Raphael Hirsch almost one hundred years ago].
Therefore resting from work means keeping the Sabbath,
doing work means desecrating it. The Law does not say
that he who does not listen to the sermon or say his prayers
has transgressed it; but it says whosoever works on the
Sabbath forfeits his life. *Issur m'lachah* — abstinence from
work, this is the sign which God expects on every Sabbath, abstinence from work is the sign by which He seeks
to prove whether we still call ourselves His. Abstinence
from work is the sign by which we are to demonstrate that
God is the Creator of heaven and earth, that He is also
our Creator and that we too belong to Him, that all powers
are His, and are consecrated to His service.

For six days the world belongs to us, for six days we
may exercise our dominion over everything that our God
has created, and perform *m'lachah;* we may stamp our
creative impress on everything and make it the agent of
our will, the executor of our purpose. But on the seventh
day we shall testify that, after all, the world is not ours,
that we are not its lord and master, but merely God's

vassal on earth, that we only live and work by God's grace, that He is our Lord and Master, the Lord and Master of the smallest as of the greatest creature within our ken. To this we shall testify by giving the world its freedom on this day, by retiring into that sphere which is subject to ourselves. . . . The bird, the fish, the animal that we refrain from seizing on the Sabbath, the plant that we refrain from tearing up, the material that we refrain from fashioning or chiselling, cutting or mixing, moulding or preparing, all this inaction is but a demonstration of homage to God, proclaiming Him Creator and Master and Lord of the world. The Jewish child who refrains from catching the butterfly or plucking the flower on the Sabbath glorifies the Almighty God more effectively than the most brilliant orators and poets glorify Him by their words and songs.

All thoughts which might lead to profaning the Sabbath but which we hold in check, so as not to make the smallest creature, the tiniest fibre of material into a servant of the least of our purposes, so as nowhere in God's world to stamp the impress of our human authority, are just so many tokens of our service to God, so many renewed tokens of our wish to fulfill our covenant with God. And the Jew whom neither the desire of pleasure nor the hope of profit, whom neither the love of comfort nor frivolity can tempt to engage in productive activity on the Sabbath has, by his self-restraint and by his consecration of his thoughts and faculties to the service of God, sanctified himself more truly than if he had shed pious tears in the Synagogue and then turned to his weekly chores.[8]

Those who love the Sabbath look upon the world with different eyes on that day, viewing it not simply as grist for their mills but as a miracle to be amazed at. Their pride quieted, nature itself seems renewed.

Thus, when the Rabbi of Rizhyn was a child, he was once walking up and down in the yard on a Friday toward evening, gazing up into the sky, long after the *hasidim* had already gone off to pray. A *hasid* went up to him and said, "Why don't you go in? The Sabbath has already begun."

"The Sabbath hasn't begun yet," he replied.

"How do you know that?" asked the *hasid.*

"On the Sabbath," he answered, "there always appears a new Heaven, and I can't see any sign of it yet."

On the Sabbath we are at peace with nature and recognize that we are not self-sufficient masters but creatures of an Almighty Creator. Thus the Sabbath brings peace between man and nature.

Peace Between Man and Society

The Sabbath brings peace *between man and society.*

All week we struggle to make a living; we fight for our social and economic existence. There is a war in every marketplace and every business is a battleground. On this day we declare an armistice. We lay down the weapons of battle. We touch no money. We withdraw from the conflict between man and man. We are free from the inequalities which our economic and social existence put upon us. We all stand as equals before God.

Remember the Sabbath day, to keep it holy. Six days shalt thou labor, and do all thy work; but the seventh day is the Sabbath of the Lord thy God; in it thou shalt not do any work, thou, nor thy son nor thy daughter, nor thy manservant, nor thy maidservant, nor thy cattle, nor thy stranger that is within thy gates (Exodus 20:8-10).

So radical was the Sabbath commandment of stopping work one day in seven that it was little understood by the ancient pagans. Even the advanced cultures of Rome and Greece found it strange. Their writers called it a "mad custom" and a "foolish practice." Seneca found it a "reprehensible Jewish superstition" which caused the Jews to "lose a seventh part of their lifetime, passing it in idleness." Juvenal agreed that it was "a day of laziness," while Rutilius wrote that "every seventh day is devoted to base inactivity — a weak reflection, so to speak, of a weary God." To their way of thinking one either worked all of the time — as did most of the population — or none of the time — as did a privileged portion of the people. To keep the Sabbath was to break with the benighted, universal practice of mankind and to strike a shattering blow for freedom and equality.

On the seventh day the manservant and maidservant and stranger — even the cattle — are no longer inferior beings. They are freed from inequality and deprecation. This is why, in Deuteronomy, the reason given for observing the Sabbath is not (as in Exodus 20:11) because "in six days the Lord made heaven and earth, the sea, and all that in them is, and rested on the seventh day; wherefore the Lord blessed the Sabbath day, and hallowed it" — that is, *because God rested;* but because "the Lord thy God brought thee out [from the land of Egypt] with a mighty hand and an outstretched arm" (Deuteronomy 5:15) — that is, *because of the exodus from Egypt.* The Sabbath is a day of freedom from slavery, both ancient and modern.

Our rest on the Sabbath is closely connected with the concept of freedom, for to be at peace with society means to be free from its shackles, not to be a slave to poverty and competition and power and strife, but to stand in equality before the Lord of all creation. Thus, when we observe the Sabbath by resting, this resting must be understood as an expression of freedom from conflict and disparity. Typical of the social legislation surrounding the Sabbath is this passage from a medieval code, *Arugat Habosem:* "One must take care to pay the teachers of one's children before each Sabbath, for there are those who say that the *neshamah yeterah* (the added soul provided by the Sabbath) is denied to one who fails to do so."

Oft repeated in poems and stories is the way in which the ghetto Jew, cursed and driven during the week as the pariah of mankind, became transformed into a king on the Sabbath, with his home a palace, his children princes, his wife a queen. But what is not so often stressed is the equality he achieved with all other Jews through the Sabbath. Although one Jew may have peddled onions and another may have owned great forests of lumber, on the Sabbath all were equal, all were kings: all welcomed the Sabbath Queen, all chanted the *Kiddush,* all basked in the glory of the seventh day. The uneven divisions of society were leveled with the setting of the sun. On the Sabbath there was neither banker nor clerk, neither farmer nor hired-hand, neither mistress nor maid, neither rich nor poor. There were only Jews hallowing the Sabbath. The carriage driver could not be ordered to wait for his master outside the synagogue to drive him home after the services; instead, both prayed together, both wore the *talit.* On the Sabbath, even the *shlemiel* is a child of God. He forgets his worries; the Sabbath redeems him from his social and economic predicament.

It is "a remembrance of the going out of Egypt," for on each Sabbath the Jew is delivered from the bondage of an Egypt not limited to any country or century, but one including every land and every age — an Egypt of business competition and struggle for power, of economic inequality and social snobbery, of rich and poor, of high and low, of the haves and have-nots, an Egypt filled with Pharaohs and taskmasters, the making of bricks and the building of pyramids, an Egypt thick with the darkness of anxiety. From all this the Sabbath liberates us once a week. Through the miracle of a day we are released from the crush of bondage.

The Sabbath is the great equalizer.

If a new Ten Commandments were to be drawn up today for twentieth century man, prominent among them would surely be a law not to touch money one day a week. How vital to our age it would be to have a day when the shopkeeper and the customer alike might be removed from all temptation to buy or sell, when no one would even think of entering a store because he could purchase nothing, and the store itself would stand closed because one could sell nothing. What a blessing it would be for modern man to have one day a week free from all commerce. But that is precisely what the Sabbath has given the Jew for centuries. The halt it brings to our economic lives is a call to sanity.

If we did not have this Sabbath, this day of rest ordained by God [writes Hirsch with a keen understanding of the challenge of modern industrial society], when would we rest, when would we come to ourself, to our wife and child, when would we attend to our mind and spirit, to our heaven upon earth? When we have time to spare? But when will we or dare we have time to spare? Incessantly is the material world around us at work. It never rests, unceasingly it struggles for its existence. Irresistibly it marches on. He who does not go forward, goes backward; he who stands still is trodden down. Could we, would we dare to cry "halt" to our labor, "halt" to our concern for our daily existence? Can we of ourselves, once caught up in the mad race, proclaim a rest for hand and head and mind, wipe away perspiration, smooth our foreheads, shake off the dust from the arena of life? Dare we once stop looking forward with earnest intent to the goal which we strive to gain, and instead look back for once, look around us and down into our inner self, look joyously and calmly at the hopes we cherish and the ideals we once strove after and have only partly realized?

Without the Sabbath, without rest, man is fated but to toil; without rest, he is tormented by worry. . . . Our fathers had to contend only with his neighbor, but we battle the whole world. Our fathers had but the village to look upon, but we set about to explore the universe. Numberless possessions and pleasures unknown to our fathers we must win for ourselves and our family by the sweat of our brow, at the highest output of our nervous system, at the greatest demand of our time. We must provide so much for ourselves and wife and child, that we have no time to think of self and wife and child. The cares of the house estrange us from the home. The word "existence" has assumed such gigantic proportions that life is entirely absorbed in the task of securing this existence, and no time is left to inquire into its purpose and aim, its value and meaning. The word "existence" has become so immense a problem that the sum total of all human wisdom, the exploration of the heavens and earth, of countries and seas, even virtue and morality, charity and benevolence, have to provide themselves with the hall-mark of economic utility in order to obtain recognition from a bread-earning humanity. And man, created to be God's image in wisdom and kindness, in love and justice, created to rejoice like God in his work, pants under the yoke of the earth, dripping with sweat, seeking for food, and no longer hears the "Where art thou?" of God's voice wandering up and down in search of him.

But then appears a messenger from Eden, the angel of God. The Sabbath approaches and says, in the name of God: No further! You must not only care for earthly bread. You sin against yourself, your wife and child if your hand is always tense only to procure food, if your foot is always moving and your mind thinking only to find a means of livelihood. Have you no heart, and dare you permit your soul to starve and wither while you keep on feeding your body? You have done enough, when you have honestly worked six days. Stop your work; enter your home with me.

You stop and listen to the words of the messenger. You breathe more calmly and begin to return to your better self. You throw off the yoke of labor, wipe the sweat from your brow and shake off the dust from your clothes. Your forehead regains its smoothness. You raise your head and look around. Now you hear the heavenly voice calling you home to your family circle, to the side of wife and children. The Sabbath comes to your soul and home; your dwelling becomes transfigured. No house is so small or poor that God's splendor does not enter with the Sabbath. The light that shines within you increases the brightness of the Sabbath-light; the peace that dwells in you flavors the Sabbath meal; care, tears, grief and sorrow, all these the Sabbath banishes from the poorest home. Sabbath has come, you must not weep! The Sabbath has balm

and comfort for all, makes all rich and equal. . . . It does
this because it bids you, in His name, to cry a halt to your
cares and labors. It shows Him to you as your Father in
heaven, the Ruler and Guide of all ages, who knows your
troubles and feels your cares.[9]

The Sabbath transforms man. He looks upon his fellow
with different eyes.

> He does not crawl or tremble before the power of man.
> The name of God has made him free, free from the fear
> of man and the worship of man. God is as near to the
> humble cottage as He is to the most magnificent mansion;
> the souls of His children in the meanest cradle are of as
> much account as the descendants of kings bedecked in
> silk. God is as near to the man of quiet, humble calling
> as He is to the much acclaimed hero. And if God is with
> him in his quiet, honest labor, what can man do to him?
>
> The name of God has made him free, free from envy
> and arrogance, hatred and enmity, revenge and violence.
> Just as he feels himself bound up with God, so he sees
> God's name stamped upon every one of his brethren.
> Hence this name draws every one near to him as his own
> brother and teaches him to regard everyone's sphere as
> a place hallowed by divine dispensation. He does not look
> down upon the poor nor envy the rich. He grudges no one
> his blessing, his share of possessions, pleasures and honors.
>
> Competition! This word of blessing and of curse which
> drives the man without a Sabbath into the sweat and dust
> of the race after fortune, which transforms the friendly
> eye that was made to smile upon every fellow-worker into
> a look of envy, which clenches in violence and treachery
> the hand that was made to grasp every fellow man's hand
> in frank and sympathetic grip, which locks up the heart
> with bolts of envy, malice and hatred — that divine-human

heart in which mercy and love should dwell, which dwarfs
the spirit that was destined to be a torch of truth and
justice into falsehood, injustice and violence; "competition" which has transformed society from a brotherhood
that rejoiced in the blessing of God into a horde of fratri-
cidal strife. But for the man who keeps the Sabbath this
same "competition" has lost its power. He has been taught
that he was not created to build his house upon the ruins
of his neighbor's fortune or to place his proud foot upon
his brother's neck. His brother's downfall cannot raise
him nor can his brother's elevation hinder him. And as
the poison of envy is driven out of the breast of the man
who keeps the Sabbath, the blossoms of love and charity
grow up in its place. . . .

By the Sabbath every human home and heart recognizes
not only the God of the universe, the God of nature, but
the God Who is ever near to every human dwelling and
heart, under Whose care every dwelling and soul reposes.
With this knowledge salvation is brought to every dwelling and peace to every soul. Give the world the Sabbath
and you will break the fetters and heal the wounds of
mankind.

To really observe the Sabbath in our day and age! To
cease for a whole day from all business, from all work,
amidst the frenzied hurry-scurry of our age! To close the
stock exchanges, the stores, the factories — how would it
be possible? The pulse of life would stop beating and the
world perish!

The world perish? On the contrary, it would be saved. . . .

The more we see how our business swallows up every
interest and the more we are caught up in the industrial
current, the more we must tremble at the thought that
we and our children may finally be completely submerged
in it, that in it we may lose our God and the whole dig-

nity of the human personality. Thus, the more important business becomes, the more precious our time becomes, the more profit and loss depends on days, hours and minutes, the stronger the industrial chain grows, the greater must our zeal be for the Sabbath, the more fervently must we grasp the Kiddush cup, the more devoutly must we gather wife and child about us and hallow the Sabbath, giving fervent thanks for its saving gift. We must teach them through self-sacrificing example . . . and by the solemnity and earnestness of our Sabbath observance that not our industry, our trade or our profession is our God and the bulwark of our life, but the Lord is our God even now, the God Who not only created the world, but Who rules it with power and governs it with blessing and Who from the days of Egypt downward has taught us to realize His power and His providence that He may remain our God and our children's God for ever and ever.[10]

Does the testimony of the contemporary American Jew confirm the rightness of Rabbi Samson Raphael Hirsch's passionate plea? Herman Wouk, best-selling novelist and Broadway playwright, answers in the affirmative:

The Sabbath has cut most sharply athwart my own life when one of my plays has been in rehearsal or in tryout. The crisis atmosphere of an attempt at Broadway is a legend of our time, and a true one; I have felt under less pressure going into battle at sea. Friday afternoon, during these rehearsals, inevitably seems to come when the project is tottering on the edge of ruin. I have sometimes felt guilty of treason, holding to the Sabbath in such a desperate situation. But then, experience has taught me that a theatre enterprise almost always is in such a case. Sometimes it does totter to ruin, and sometimes it totters to great prosperity, but tottering is its normal gait, and cries of anguish are its normal tone of voice. So I have reluctantly taken leave of my colleagues on Friday afternoon, and rejoined them on Saturday night. The play has never yet collapsed in the meantime. When I return I find it tottering as before, and the anguished cries as normally despairing as ever. My plays have encountered in the end both success and failure, but I cannot honestly ascribe either result to my observing the Sabbath.

Leaving the gloomy theatre, the littered coffee cups, the jumbled scarred-up scripts, the haggard actors, the shouting stagehands, the bedevilled director, the knuckle-gnawing producer, the clattering typewriter, and the dense tobacco smoke and backstage dust, I have come home. It has been a startling change, very like a brief return from the wars. My wife and my boys, whose existence I have almost forgotten in the anxious shoring up of the tottering ruin, are waiting for me, gay, dressed in holiday clothes, and looking to be marvelously attractive. We have sat down to a splendid dinner, at a table graced with flowers and the old Sabbath symbols: the burning candles, the twisted loaves, the stuffed fish, and my grandfather's silver goblet brimming with wine. I have blessed my boys with the ancient blessing: we have sung the pleasantly syncopated Sabbath table hymns. The talk has had little to do with tottering ruins. My wife and I have caught up with our week's conversation. The boys, knowing that the Sabbath is the occasion for asking questions, have asked them. The Bible, the encyclopedia, the atlas, have piled up on the table. We talk of Judaism, and there are the usual impossible boys' queries about God, which my wife and I field clumsily but as well as we can. For me it is a retreat into restorative magic.

Saturday has passed in much the same manner. The

boys are at home in the synagogue, and they like it. They like even more the assured presence of their parents. In the weekday press of schooling, household chores and work — and especially in a play-producing time — it often happens that they see little of us. On the Sabbath we are always there, and they know it. They know too that I am not working, and that my wife is at her ease. It is their day.

It is my day, too. The telephone is silent. I can think, read, study, walk, or do nothing. It is an oasis of quiet. When night falls, I go back to the wonderful nerve-racking Broadway game. Often I make my best contribution of the week then and there to the grisly literary surgery that goes on and on until opening night. My producer one Saturday night said to me, "I don't envy you your religion, but I envy you your Sabbath." [11]

A gentile reporter, after her first visit to Israel, observed in a popular magazine that "the official beginning of the Sabbath is at sunset the previous evening, and a notice in the Friday paper tells exactly what time it is. After you've been through a few of them you can see why. They don't just close the stores; they shut down the whole city. Now that I'm used to it, I'm all for it and think if they'd shut down the whole world one day a week, we wouldn't be in the mess we're in." [12]

On the Sabbath there is peace between man and society.

Peace Between Man and Himself

The Sabbath brings peace *between man and himself*.
Having made peace with the conflicts that rage *about* us — both with nature, of whose true Lord Sabbath ob-

servance teaches us, and with society, of whose true purpose Sabbath rest makes us aware — it is easier for us
to make peace with the strife that burns *within* us.

Who among us is without personal problems? Where
is the man who harbors no private grief, the woman
who wastes no time in worry? Age is no exemption, and
sex only varies the ailment and the pain. Scratch the skin
of any of us — no matter the outer calm, the deep tan,
the display of success — and you will find anxiety, suffering, torment.

Man is half-animal, half-angel, and for six days there
is a struggle between the two. One day a week, however,
we learn how to make peace between body and soul, between spirit and flesh. The Sabbath teaches us that the
conflicting drives which beset man need not be contra-
dictory, that the spirit need not battle with the flesh,
and that, with the help of God and His creation, the
conflict may be overcome. The Sabbath reconciles, shows
us how to enlist the desires of the body and turn them
to noble ends, how to capture the "evil urge" and bring
it under the realm of the holy, how to sanctify the common. For the Sabbath is not a day for the soul alone;
it was meant for the body as well. "And Moses said, 'Eat
it today, for a Sabbath is this day unto the Lord' " (Exodus 16:25). Rabbi Zerika, a Talmudic sage, explains
this verse to mean that from this we learn "that one
should have three meals on the Sabbath" (Shabbat 117b).
Holiness does not mean removal from the world but
sanctification of the worldly. We are not required to
become ascetics on the Seventh Day; our physical demands are not denied. What happens, however, is that
on the Sabbath, these physical demands become *mitzvot,*

and are transformed into something in which God too has a share, in which there is divine concern. Food, wine, marital relations, all of them fleshly desires, become *mitzvot* on the Sabbath. Thus the passions are sanctified, the "evil urge" is transformed and enlisted in the divine cause.

This is why

We greet each other on the Sabbath with the words, *Shabbat Shalom* — a Sabbath of peace. For during the week, concord between the body and the soul is lacking. If one partakes of a tasty meal, the body rejoices but the soul laments; while if one busies himself with Torah, prayer or good deeds, the soul rejoices but the body complains. On the Sabbath day, however, all is different. The soul does not object when the body delights in good food, sleep and the like, since on that day they are *mitzvot;* while the body accedes to the soul's devotion to Torah and prayer, since the claims of one's work is then gone. As body and soul dwell at peace with one another, we say *"Shabbat Shalom!"*

A parable. Once there was a man whose first wife died after bearing him a son. He married a woman whose first husband had died after she had borne him a daughter. There was dissension between them. He was as jealous of the attention she gave her daughter as she was of the favors he showed his son. In time, the children grew up and married one another. This marriage brought harmony to the lives of the parents. Now he wished his wife to dote on her daughter, for was she not married to his son? And she urged her husband to be generous with his son, for was he not married to her daughter?

So it is that on the weekday there is strife between body and soul, for each is jealous of the attentions shown the other. But on the Sabbath the tension between them ceases, for they are wedded one to the other: the soul rejoicing in the delights of the body and the body delighting in the rejoicing of the soul. Thus does one Jew greet his neighbor on the Sabbath with the words: *Shabbat Shalom!*[13]

Likewise, the desire to hurt and to hamper, the urge to shame and destroy, is lessened on the Sabbath. The evil within us which we more freely express during the other six days of the week is, curiously, somehow restrained, gradually overcome, through the pattern of holiness which pervades the Seventh Day. Welcoming the Sabbath Bride-Queen, going to the synagogue, opening our hearts to God in prayer, listening to the ancient words of the Torah and their application to our time and our lives, sitting together with the family around a table hallowed and sanctified and filled with Sabbath joy — all this makes it easier — at least one day a week — to be what we should be rather than what we want to be, and what we could be rather than what we often are. Even the humblest home had its Sabbath guest — the stranger or the needy or the lonely — with whom it shared its meager food, a weekly lesson on kindness to every member of the family. On the Sabbath it is difficult to take revenge, to tell a lie, to hurt, to shame, to be ungrateful, to hate, to be angry, to betray, to sin, to carouse, to be indecent; it is easier to forgive, to speak the truth, to show pity, to have respect, to love, to be gentle, to be grateful, to be loyal, to be modest. The commandment, " 'Ye shall kindle no fire throughout your habitations on the Sabbath Day' (Exodus 35:3), is interpreted to mean: 'Ye shall kindle no fire of controversy nor the heat of anger.' Ye shall kindle no fire — not even the fire of righteous indignation."[14] It is as if the *neshamah yeterah* (the added soul the Jew receives on the Sabbath) joins the soul we already have and succeeds in quieting all evil, encouraging all thoughts and deeds of goodness.

On the Sabbath a clearly visible change takes place in the Jew who loves and keeps it. The words of the prophet, ". . . honor the Sabbath by not going about your accustomed ways" (Isaiah 58:13), was explained by the Rabbis (Shabbat 113a) to mean, "that your habits on the Sabbath should be different from those on the weekday: your gait on the Sabbath should not be as on the weekday; your clothes on the Sabbath should not be as on the weekday; your food on the Sabbath should not be as on the weekday." Thus there came to be a special Sabbath stride — the most leisurely; a special Sabbath food — the tastiest; a special Sabbath dress — the finest; a special Sabbath table — the loveliest. In all things, great and small, the Sabbath has cast its sway. In the early 1930's, Rabbi Leo Baeck of Berlin once went on a trip to Chicago, a city quite strange to him. He planned to attend a certain synagogue on Sabbath afternoon, but soon he lost his way. "Then I saw a Jew," he said, "and I knew at once that this man was going to *Minhah*. Without speaking to him, I followed him, and he proceeded slowly and calmly, until I arrived safely at the Synagogue."

The outer transformation which comes over the Jew on the Sabbath, however, is but the vesture of a deeper, inner renewal that permeates his very being. Among the most profound explanations of this phenomenon was that of Rabbi Levi Yitzhak of Berditchev. Taking the word

Shabbat from *shuv*, which means "to turn," he explained that "on the Sabbath man turns back to his true self." He becomes, in other words, what he was meant to be. Shorn of competition and the need to create, he is able to gather the spiritual sources of his life once again into their primeval whole. "On the Sabbath day," Franz Rosenzweig wrote, "the Jew becomes another person. The crown 'man' is once again set upon his brow. His lost dignity returns. With the worries of the week go the feelings of the weekday. He is raised out of the narrowness of his daily life to become the Sabbath Jew. The thread of mercy returns. It is as before the poison of the serpent came into the world." [15]

One of the striking features of the change which the Sabbath has wrought upon the Jew is an alteration of his pattern of speech. One's words on the Sabbath are to be fewer and more choice. In many homes only the holy tongue was employed, and certainly all talk of business and the like was avoided. It was as if one were striving more to hear on this day than to speak, to create less and listen for the Creator more.

> Six days man has worked and attended to all his affairs; now, on the seventh, he rests. Six days he has uttered the many useful and useless things the workday demanded of him, but on the seventh he obeys the command of the prophet; he lets his tongue rest from the talk of everyday, and learns to be silent, to listen. And this sanctifying of the day of rest by listening to God's voice in silence must be shared by all members of his house. It must not be fretted by the noise of giving orders. The man-servant and the maid-servant must also rest; and it is even said that just for the sake of their rest the day of rest was instituted,

for when rest has penetrated to them, then all the house is, indeed, freed from the noise and chatter of the weekday, and redeemed to rest.[16]

To learn to listen to the voice that can only be perceived once the din of the weekday subsides is a special blessing of the Jewish Sabbath. One of the great critics of contemporary society, Lewis Mumford, a gentile, appreciates the unique value in this withdrawal once a week from the active, divisive life, which so dulls the senses, to a more passive mode of living which permits new sounds to be heard and new experiences to be felt.

The first public acknowledgment of the need for a creative pause was, of course, the Jewish institution of the Sabbath: a social invention of the first magnitude. But in our western culture the day of rest has now become another day of busy work, filled with amusements and restless diversions not essentially different from the routine of the workweek — particularly in America: from the Sunday morning scramble through the metropolitan newspaper to the distracting tedium of the motor car excursion, we continually activate leisure time, instead of letting all work and routine duties come serenely to a halt. Even in Wordsworth's day, the pressure to be up and doing must have been heavy; why, otherwise, his lines: "Think you, mid all this mighty sum of things for ever speaking, that nothing of itself will come, but we must still be seeking?" That wise passiveness in which the soul lies open to whatever forces from any direction may touch it is a highly necessary counterpoise to over-narrowed and over-directed forms of activity, particularly to drilled submission to the machine.

Each member of the household experiences the magic

of the Sabbath in a different way: the children, free from the tension of school and weekday chores, dress in their Sabbath finery and look forward to being with mother and father in a festive, leisurely setting, an occasion to talk of all the things that have been stored up during the week; the father, after tiring and hectic days at the office, finds the Sabbath a retreat of quiet and a time for family enrichment and spiritual nurture; and the mother — but something more needs to be said of her. The mother has always been associated in a special way with the idea of the Sabbath. The very terms, Bride and Queen, by which the day is called are feminine. Indeed, the Sabbath has been referred to as the "perennial Mother's Day of the Jew." For she is the one who, in kindling the lights, perhaps the most symbolic act of the Sabbath, not only inaugurates the day, but casts a mood of holiness and splendor through the entire house. It was this very act which so impressed the Roman women of antiquity that many converted to emulate her. The mother is able to create a new mood precisely because a new mood is created within her each Sabbath. "The author, Sholem Asch, has described the transformation of the poor, tired, shabby, weekday-mother of little Yechiel into another mother, a radiant Sabbath-mother 'with infinite maternal loveliness shining from her face, her eyes, her brow, which gleamed like the sun.' But there never was a Jewish mother, how humble or high her daily standard, how much she might have been debased or elevated by her fate, who has not experienced the transfiguration of Yechiel's mother. For to every Jewish mother every Sabbath is a source of revival and sanctification." [17]

A mood of Sabbath peace, Israel Zangwill tells us, descended upon the whole Jewish community of the past. "The roaring Sambatyon of life was at rest in the Ghetto; on thousands of squalid homes the light of Sinai shone. The Ghetto welcomed the Sabbath Bride with proud song and humble feast, and sped her parting with optimistic symbolisms of fire and wine, of spice and light and shadow. All around their neighbours sought distraction in the blazing public houses, and their tipsy bellowings resounded through the streets and mingled with the Hebrew hymns. Here and there the voice of a beaten woman rose on the air. But no Son of the Covenant was among the revellers or the wife-beaters; the Jews remained a chosen race, a peculiar people, faulty enough, but redeemed at least from the grosser vices — a little human islet won from the waters of animalism by the genius of ancient engineers."

But we need not turn nostalgically to the ghettos of the past for a picture of the miracle the Sabbath can bring into the life of the Jew. The modern State of Israel is the supreme example. For many visitors, the experience of the Sabbath is the highlight of their trip. Early Friday, the community is in a bustle: porches are swept, the smell of fresh *chalah* is in the air, the stores are crowded. Towards the afternoon the mood changes: shops begin to close, men hasten home from work with flowers in their hands, last minute chores are completed. At twilight the Sabbath descends upon the city, now clean, quiet and ready, in all her radiant glory. The reign of the Queen has cleared the way for the Bride. Quiet joy. Candles flickering. Devout prayer. Soft laughter. Happy faces. Friendly talk. Families united in Sabbath peace.

The *menuhah* of the Sabbath means in its deepest sense an inner harmony. One day a week we make peace with ourselves.

The Victory of the Sabbath

The seventh day is the armistice in man's cruel struggle for existence, a truce in all conflicts, personal and social, peace between man and man, man and nature, peace within man; a day on which handling money is considered a desecration, on which man avows his independence of that which is the world's chief idol. The seventh day is the exodus from tension, the liberation of man from his own muddiness, the installation of man as a sovereign in the world of time.

In the tempestuous ocean of time and toil there are islands of stillness where man may enter a harbor and reclaim his dignity. The island is the seventh day, the Sabbath, a day of detachment from things, instruments and practical affairs as well as of attachment to the spirit. . . . The Sabbath, thus, is more than an armistice, more than an interlude; it is a profound, conscious harmony of man and the world, a sympathy for all things and a participation in the spirit that unites what is below and what is above. All that is divine in the world is brought into union with God. . . .

To set apart one day a week for freedom, a day on which we would not use the instruments which have been so easily turned into weapons of destruction, a day for being with ourselves, a day of detachment from the vulgar, of independence of external obligations, a day on which we stop worshipping the idols of technical civilization, a day on which we use no money, a day of armistice in the economic struggle with our fellow men and the forces of nature — is there any institution that holds out a greater hope for man's progress than the Sabbath?[18]

On all three levels then — with nature around us, our fellow man beside us and our own selves within us — the Sabbath brings peace to the constant struggle which all of life engenders. The greeting of the Sabbath is *"Shabbat Shalom,"* "a Sabbath of peace," of unity and harmony and wholeness, a bringing together again what for six days is shattered and broken and split. Even the Sabbath angels who are supposed to visit each Jewish home are called "angels of peace." It is peace which characterizes the Sabbath in our relations to ourselves, our society and all of nature. It is a sense of peace which is both a memory of the original harmony that existed in the Garden of Eden before man was cursed with enmity and conflict and a foretaste of the ultimate harmony which will reign once again at the end of time. Within history, the Sabbath is "a foretaste of the future world." But, paradoxically, to describe the future world itself, our sages must refer back to the Sabbath. They call it "the time which is all-Sabbath." What will the future world be like? It will be one great Sabbath. It is not only that the Sabbath draws from heaven; heaven too draws from the Sabbath.

> At the time of the giving of the Torah, the Holy One blessed-be-He, called Israel to Him and said:
>
> "My children, if you will accept my Torah and keep my commandments, I have a precious reward for you."
>
> "Master of the world," they replied, "what is this reward you have for us?"
>
> "Paradise."
>
> "Show us something of it."
>
> God showed them the Sabbath.[19]

If the Sabbath is the symbol of ultimate harmony, a cessation of all conflict, an aspect of heaven, a foretaste of the next world, why should it be limited to one day out of seven? This question made itself felt in our fore-fathers' very style of living, for the love for the Sabbath was so great among the people of Israel that the bounds of twenty-four hours could no longer contain it. Its coming was — and still is — anticipated, awaited with eagerness. Candles are lit and the home is prepared before the sun sets. We have not only *Shabbat* but *Erev Shabbat,* which takes on much of the holiness of the Sabbath itself, for the Law states that on Friday afternoon only the most necessary work should be done. Thus additional hours are added to the beginning of the Sabbath. Just as the Sabbath is welcomed early and eagerly, so is it relinquished tardily and reluctantly. The Sabbath does not end precisely at sunset but only with the appearance of three stars in the sky. (Among some Jews it ends even later.) The *Hasidim,* in their farewell, chant songs without words until long after darkness has fallen, songs which melt the soul with their yearning and longing, for it is at the moment of the Bride's departure that the heart is most open.

There were epochs in Jewish history when the Sabbath moved from the end of the week, one day after six, to its very center, the hub of time's wheel. The Sabbath was like the ancient seven-branched *Menorah* that stood in the Temple, whose middle member rose from the base, towering above and radiating light upon the other six, which faced it three by three. Thus did Rabbi Noah of Lekhovitz explain the difference between the two Sabbath commandments in Exodus and Deuteronomy.

"*Zakhor* means *remember* the Sabbath, even until three days after it has passed. *Shamor* means *watch for* the Sabbath, even three days before it comes."[20]

According to the mystics, one should keep the Sabbath as if it would never end. So it sometimes happened to the holy men of Israel, when the time came to kindle the *Havdalah* light on Saturday night, marking the close of the Sabbath, that surprise and confusion would overcome them. They dreaded to encounter the weekday, which they had dared to hope would never again return. In despair they prayed:

"Behold, Thou art the God of my salvation.

I shall put my trust in Thee and have no fear!"

There are those in our day, innocent of the beauty of the Sabbath, who, in failing to make *Kiddush* on Friday evening, promote a secular, weekday ("wochedic") world. But there are others in whom there still burns the old Jewish yearning for a time that will be only Sabbath. They are like the Rabbi in Peretz's play who, refusing to make *Havdalah* one Saturday night because he wanted a world that was all Sabbath ("Shabbosdic"), cried out: "*Shabbos zoll zein oif der velt!*"

If we are able to feel the power and grandeur and peace of the Sabbath one day a week, learning to mend our tattered souls and join flesh and spirit in joy and rest, in inward feeling and outward act, perhaps we shall be able to bring a portion of the spirit of this day into the other days of the week, so that even the ordinary weekday will take on something of the Sabbath. It is the conquest of the six days by the Seventh Day, and victory of the holy over the profane, the dominion of the sacred over the common, which is the ultimate goal of human

history, the final vision of the prophets and the promise
of the Eternal. "If Israel would only keep the Sabbath
for two weeks," say the Rabbis (Shabbat 118b), "the
Messiah would come."

The children of Israel *shall* keep the Sabbath,
To observe the Sabbath throughout their generations
As an eternal covenant.
It is a sign between Me and them
Forever (Exodus 31:16-17).

IV

From Understanding to Doing

Mind and Will

So far we have discussed the meaning of the Sabbath.
We have learned how the Jew was able to turn a day
into a person — the Bride-Queen — who brought peace
to all three levels of his conflict: with nature, society and
himself. Impressive as this argument is, it addresses itself primarily to the mind and heart. Appreciation of
what the Sabbath meant for our ancestors in days gone
by — and what it still means for many of our fellow Jews
today — is not enough. Most of us, through no fault of
our own, are strangers to the weekly rhythm of Sabbath
observance, and, at best, still stand as admiring out-
siders looking in. How do we go from "understanding"
to "doing"? How can our will turn what we know is
right and feel is true into daily deeds of life?

The Sabbath in Jewish History

To help us reach a decision about the Sabbath, it might be well to review the unwavering resolution Jews expressed for the Sabbath throughout their history. The Talmud (Shabbat 130a) relates that the most precious *mitzvot* are those for which the people of Israel are willing to give up their lives. Pre-eminent among them is the Sabbath. Knowing that the Sabbath was a source of unique strength to the people Israel, the Romans, the Nazis, and others forbade (the Russians still virtually forbid) its observance. Yet there were then, as there are now, Jews who have persisted in keeping it. Because it was seen as the very essence of their faith, Jews gladly sacrificed for it, and, in doing so, it became ever dearer to them. Let us cite several examples:

The first is from the Maccabean and Roman wars, during which our people at first refused to fight on the Sabbath, an advantage the enemy used to its benefit. In I Maccabees we read:

> . . . They [the Syrians] encamped against them [the Jews], and set the battle in array against them on the Sabbath day. . . . And they [the Jews] said, "We will not come forth to profane the Sabbath day." And they hasted to give them battle. And they answered them not. . . . And they died, they and their wives and their children, to the number of a thousand souls.[21]

Israel's losses became so great that at last they were forced to defend themselves on that day. Still they refused to attack! But "so long as the heathen could assault the Jews on the Sabbath with impunity, just so long was the possibility of national independence out of the question.''[22] How dear the Sabbath must have been to those brave warriors if they were willing to sacrifice victory and independence for it, allowing themselves at times to be slaughtered, and what troubled thoughts must have preceded the decision to forsake part of the Torah that the Torah itself might be preserved. Later, in the Roman period, this decision to defend themselves on the Sabbath but not to attack placed the Jews in mortal danger. Thus Josephus describes the siege of Jerusalem by Pompey:

> The Torah permits us to defend ourselves against those who begin a battle and strike us, but it does not allow us to fight against an enemy that does nothing else. Of this fact the Romans were well aware, and on those days which we call the Sabbath, they did not shoot at the Jews or meet them in hand to hand combat, but instead they raised earthworks and towers, and brought up their siege-engines in order that these might be put to work the following day.[23]

During the Middle Ages the secret Jews of Spain, called the Marranos, living in fear of their lives, tried to keep the Sabbath day holy. Knowing this, the leaders of the Inquisition directed their agents to ascend to the roof of the tallest building in the winter on Sabbath days and scan the city to see if any chimney failed to emit smoke, the sign, perhaps, of a cryptic Jew; or to suddenly break into a suspected Jewish home on Friday night to learn if a festive meal were in progress or Sabbath candles had been lit, even in the cellar, as was the practice among the Marranos. Despite centuries of persecution, traces of Sabbath observance have persisted among them until our day.

Turning to modern times, the writer Anzia Yezierska gives another example, recording a vivid memory of the New York's East Side at the turn of the century.

> As I neared the house we lived in, I paused terror stricken. On the sidewalk stood a jumbled pile of ragged house-furnishings that looked familiar — chairs, dishes, kitchen pans. Amidst bundles of bedding and broken furniture stood my mother. Oblivious of the curious crowd, she lit the Sabbath candles and prayed over them. In a flash I understood it all. Because of the loss of my wages while I was in the hospital, we had been evicted for unpaid rent. It was Sabbath eve. My father was in the synagogue praying and my mother, defiant of disgrace, had gone on with the ceremony of the Sabbath. All the romance of our race was in the light of those Sabbath candles. Homeless, abandoned by God and man, yet in the very desolation of the streets my mother's faith burned — a challenge to all America.[24]

Finally, an example from the Holocaust. This is a story that was written down by a victim of the concentration camps who survived and who now lives in Israel.

In 1943 he, his brothers and his mother were imprisoned in the ghetto of Kovno. One of the things which kept them alive was the Sabbath, which they clung to with all their strength. Each week when the Sabbath came and the lights were kindled, the songs sung and the prayers recited, new life entered the souls of the Jews. The Nazis understood the power of the Sabbath among the Jews and set out to destroy it in a typically clever way. They gave the Jews their week's supply of food on Sunday, figuring that they would surely devour the small portion of bread in the first few days of the week so they would have nothing to eat by the time the Sabbath came. But the Nazis did not reckon on the power and the piety of the Jewish woman. Now read the story as the son tells what happened:

The older members of our family learned to discipline themselves and to divide their bread into a portion for each day, but the undernourished, famished children would cling to the mother pleading:

"Mother, we are not able to break this bread into pieces, one for each day, Mother, you do it for us!"

And so my mother, that most unfortunate of all creatures, bore with what courage and strength she had the burden of the family, and she divided the bread into pieces, one for each day. It was not easy work. She divided the bread into the smallest pieces possible, trying to make the portions as alike as she could and worrying in the moment of decision how she might be able to set aside something — no matter how little — for the coming of the Sabbath.

"Remember, children, the days pass swiftly. The holy Sabbath approaches and knocks upon the door! Remember, for the sake of God's name!"

But the mother's heart — a merciful heart — knew what a trial it would be for the children to put aside their bread and not eat it all up until the end of the week. So she took upon herself also the task of keeping the bread.

"Listen, children! The pieces of bread which are for the Sabbath I shall keep for you. Let each of you give me as much as you like *l'kovod Shabbos* and I shall keep it!"

"Yes, yes. That is best, Mother!" Many voices spoke at once.

But one of the children who lay on a sickbed, hesitated and called out in a shy voice: "If we all give bread for *Shabbos,* Mother, will you make a good *kugel* for this

Shabbos for us like you did last *Shabbos?*"

"If God wills it! If God wills it!" answered the Mother
in a whispered prayer.

"That was wonderful *kugel.* How was it prepared? Tell
us, Mother!" said one of the children, who remembered
its taste from the week before.

"Secrets like that cannot be told, children!" The mother
smiled.

She knew only too well the hidden secret of the *kugel*'s
preparation, and it filled her with shame now. She did
not reveal her secret. What was there to reveal? Should
she tell them that from her own portion of that cursed
bread she had taken a bit each day and that from these
bits came the wonderful *kugel* — but that now her youngest child was sick and each day she gave him part of her
own bread, so she could no longer set aside anything for
a pie?

"This *Shabbos* too, dear children, you will eat good
kugel, if God wills it!" she said, taking the pieces of bread
from the children, and placing them with trembling hands
onto the white *Shabbos* tablecloth.

"I promise you that this will be a good pie, an especially good one, children!"

She had made a promise — and she fulfilled it.

Indeed, a Sabbath *kugel* the like of this one had never
yet been made. She gathered together potato peelings and
carefully hid them away. When no one was looking, she
soaked them in water and cleansed them so that no dirt
remained upon them. After they had dried, she ground
them in her bare hands. Into this flour she put salt,
pepper, a little bit of bran and grass. And to this strange
mixture there was added for spice — a mother's hot
tears. . . .

"May it be His will" — she whispered in her heart a

prayer as she worked — "May it be His will that this food will be sweet to my dear children, and that they may find in it the taste of the manna from heaven just as our fathers did in the wilderness. And may it be Thy will, O Master of the world, that I should not bring disgrace, God forbid, by the work of my hands to Your holy Sabbath. . . ."

All the while this humble creature labored preparing the pie, a single thought pursued her like a bee!

"Who knows? Perhaps — God forbid — this is a profanation of the Sabbath, a pie made of such refuse, of potato peelings. . . . Perhaps, she thought in her heart, I should add to this strange mixture some drops of oil? They will surely give it a flavor!"

But if she were to take the few remaining drops of oil for the pie what would she use to kindle her lights for *Shabbos?* For she had no candles: only wicks and oil.

A struggle went on within her soul. Food or lights? Both of them for the honor of the Sabbath: Which was more important? For a moment she thought:

"Surely the Sabbath lights take precedence, for must we not say the blessing to kindle the Sabbath lights? It is a *mitzvah* for which there is a special blessing."

A moment later she repented, saying to herself:

"What good will this light do for my sick boy who lies upon his couch? His very life hangs in the balance. A pie mixed with a little oil may give him strength; it will be good medicine for him."

Then her heart trembled within her:

"But the *mitzvah* of kindling the light may also be beneficial for my sick boy. For the child is dependent on Heaven's mercies, and there is no more favorable time for a Jewish woman to offer a prayer before the throne of glory than at the time of candlelighting."

Food or lights — what should she do?

At that moment a thought came to her mind, a daring thought:

"I will bless the Sabbath lights — without oil! And He Who dwells in the heavens and Who knows all the thoughts of man will look into my heart and He will understand. He will know that I have used the last drops of oil for the honor of the Sabbath, and to save a human life. He will forgive."

And so it happened that at the sunset of that Sabbath Eve in the Kovno ghetto she stood in front of her "lights" — singed wicks without a drop of oil — put her hands over her eyes, and recited the blessing and whispered a prayer:

"Master of all worlds! Accept my Sabbath lights which have no light. May You in Your great mercy kindle them with Your heavenly flame. Our Father in Heaven, forgive a sinful, shamed woman for having stolen the oil for the wicks in order to kindle the joy of the Sabbath in the hearts of my children, who are wasting away before my eyes. And if I am not worthy and my prayer returns empty before You, then turn Your ear, O merciful Father, to the songs of the holy Sabbath which my children — among them even my sick one — will sing in my humble dwelling when I put on the table the Sabbath *kugel* which I have made."

The *kugel* was brought to the table. The children tasted in it the taste of paradise, and they sang in a joyous chorus:

Mizmor shir leyom haShabbos!! — "A song for the Sabbath day!"

And my mother? She swallowed her tears, and did not even notice that in that dingy ghetto room the Sabbath Queen in all her glory and in all her beauty was spreading her white, radiant wings over the singing Sabbath children, and was herself singing a song to the same melody:

Mizmor shir l'eyshes hayil! — "A song of glory to the Jewish Mother!"

Is America Different?

Because the Sabbath had the power to preserve the Jew in time of peril, bringing renewal every seven days, the enemies of Israel throughout the ages — in Egypt, Rome, Germany, Russia — have attempted to halt its observance in order to crush the spirit of the people. But everywhere and always the Jewish spirit has triumphed. Everywhere, that is, but America. For America is different! This may very well be the first time in Jewish history when the total Sabbath day, for which Jews willingly made every manner of sacrifice in whatever clime or country they have lived, has been accepted as expendable. See the paradox — what our forefathers were willing to die for when it was forbidden (or at the very least made exceedingly difficult), we dismiss now that we are free to keep it. Only in America, the "goldene medinah," was the immigrant Jew too hard put economically to observe the Sabbath.

If it is true that the Sabbath is the single most important institution of Jewish life and law, if it does indeed contain within itself all of Judaism in miniature, and if it is a fact that without the Sabbath our tradition cannot endure, then how has it been permitted to fall into virtual obsolescence in America? Our continued coexistence with a Sabbath-less Jewry may blur our understanding of how radically new is the situation which confronts us in the American Jewish community. There is little awareness left of the total Sabbath in many congregations. I do not mean an informed keeping of each

and every Sabbath law, but at the very least an understanding that Sabbath observance, in the sense of withdrawal from weekday concerns and attachment to the
spiritual, as a significant and central goal for American
Jews. Few are the congregations, for example, where
Sabbath observance or even regular attendance on Sabbath morning is expected of men and women who hold
office in that congregation.

It is claimed that modern times present implacable
obstacles before Sabbath observance. Is this really so?
Of course, there are problems today that did not exist
in the insulated ghetto of yesterday. But how can one
explain the fact that in some communities today the
synagogues are very well attended on Sabbath morning
and Jews keep the Sabbath, while in other communities
the reverse is the case. A study of such communities will
disclose that those who keep the Sabbath do not hold
jobs different in kind from those who do not. The reason
must be sought elsewhere.

We have made a tragic blunder by excusing Sabbath
violation in the name of financial need, a shibboleth
that has paralyzed our attempts to apply the Sabbath
commandment to the American Jew. An unpleasant fact
must be faced: there is simply no correlation — as some
believed there was — between greater leisure or financial
well-being and Sabbath observance! The reverse is often
the case. Though we are no longer poverty-stricken im-
migrants and leisure time is heavy on our hands, it has
made little difference. If Jews wanted to keep the Sabbath, many, if not most, could.

The Jewish professional determines his own hours
and could shift his Wednesday afternoon off to Saturday.

The Jewish manufacturer and those associated with manufacturing usually work a five-day week. The Jewish retailer is in a more difficult position. Yet those who close their stores on Sabbath and holidays (and perhaps remain open on Sunday) find the reward well worth the sacrifice. There are others who are dependent upon their employers' terms. Most employees, however, will be surprised at the acceptance with which their Sabbath requests are met. Employers know that a man sincere in his religion usually makes a good worker. Further, special Jewish vocational and employment agencies are available, and fair employment laws forbidding discrimination against Sabbath observers have done much to ease the situation in recent years.

We are not helpless victims of economic laws. That would be Marxism. Jews have traditionally subjugated the law of man to the law of God which is in truth the very law of man.

Shall we give up the Sabbath? Shall we do without it for a little more comfort, a little greater affluence?

Once there was a home in which there lived seven sisters. Six worked and one cared for the house. She kept it clean and neat, so that when the others came home, it was ready for them. Though they earned a good salary and all went well, the six were not satisfied. Knowing that if their sister worked too, they would earn even more, they convinced her to do so. Now all seven worked. But no one looked after the house. In time it's lovely appearance was replaced by litter and disorder. At last the sisters saw the folly of their ways, for while their income had increased a fraction, their home was dirty, and their increased wealth was to no purpose.

So it is with our abandoning the Sabbath.

Make a Beginning

An ancient folk tale handed down from the days of the Talmud tells of a miraculous river in some far-off country that keeps the Sabbath. Sambatyon is its name. Six days a week its waters rush on, casting up rocks into the air and making a great tumult. But with the setting sun on the eve of the seventh day, the noise ceases, the water subsides and it fulfills the Sabbath command as strictly as any pious Jew.

If, instead of the Hudson, the Ohio, the Missouri, or whatever river flows through or by your city, the Sambatyon did, I have no doubt that Jews, impressed by the example of nature itself, would follow its lead, close their shops and keep the Sabbath. But "God does not give signs like these. Apparently He fears the inevitable result; the more enslaved, timid and meager the soul, the more devout. It appears that God desires for His own only the free."[25] Surely, if we were living in the ghetto where everyone kept the Sabbath, we would too. But we do not live in a society where the natural world, the human world, or even the Jewish world rests on the Sabbath, providing a genial climate of approval and encouragement. Our Sabbath must be in spite of, not because of, the world, the free choice of free men who seek their own authenticity.

Perhaps we can draw a lesson from German Jewry. They faced Western civilization with all its allurements and problems one hundred years before us. It is instructive to learn what happened to them. The emancipation of the Jews into European society brought in its wake the tragic cycles of intermarriage, conversion and self-hatred. Then in the first part of the twentieth century, significant numbers began to return. The promises for which many had forsaken their faith — that science would solve all problems, that the rule of reason would ban war forever, that man would rule in place of God — had crumbled to ashes. War, tyranny, and the rise of the demonic had shattered nineteenth century utopianism. If God had died, as Nietzsche claimed in the nineteenth century, then man who thought he replaced God, has died in the twentieth century. Many Jews who had rejected Judaism for the new messiah of Western civilization were no longer sure of themselves and were willing to give their old faith a new hearing. Men like Franz Rosenzweig, Martin Buber, Ernst Simon, Nehemiah Noble, and Hermann Cohen began to turn German Jewry back. What they began with first was the Sabbath. "If one wishes to serve God but does not know how to begin, it is best to start with the Sabbath, of which the Scripture says: 'It is first among the holy days.' "[26] A number of German Jews, persons of worldly knowledge and achievement, began to find in it blessings beyond measure and, by its light, made their way step by step. Basic, for them and for us, was what Franz Rosenzweig wrote in his famous letter to Rudolph Hallo, that for the modern Jew observance can no longer be a matter of "the all or the nothing, but rather of the something." "One only has to start," he said; "nobody can tell where this beginning will lead."

Hitler prevented our knowing what the results of German Jewry's return would have been.

After the war, Rabbi Leo Baeck, who had gone to the

concentration camp with his community rather than abandon it for freedom, visited America. He was asked by a reporter what advice he would give to American Jewry, which seemed so assimilated and removed from the Sabbath and other practices. His answer was simple: "Make a beginning."

That beginning must be through the Sabbath.

The Sabbath is the only holiday mentioned in the Ten Commandments. If the Ten Commandments contain all of the Torah, as the Rabbis say, then the Sabbath contains the entire Ten Commandments. Indeed, it is "equal to all of the other *mitzvot*." Were we to observe nothing else but the Sabbath, not even Yom Kippur or Passover, we could still live as Jews. But if we lose the Sabbath, can the Jewish people persevere?

The truth is that America is not different. American Jewry faces the same economic challenge that millions of Jews have known in the past. Indeed, financial problems have been considerably reduced for many by the five-day week and the financial success which many have achieved. What is really lacking is not so much a congenial economic environment — we have lacked that for a long time now and have still kept the Sabbath — but the conviction that the Sabbath is valuable enough to keep, even though it means a sacrifice. And it is in this respect, and not that of economics, that America has been different from Jewish communities in the past.

We need to rid ourselves of our defeatist mentality. The Sabbath was kept amidst foreign cultures in Babylonia, Spain, Italy, and Germany. It can be kept — in some ways it may be easier to keep — in America. For some, the obstacles are few; for others they are many.

For none, however, are they insurmountable — if there is the desire. Only from a conviction of the value of the Sabbath will there follow a willingness to keep it. Keeping the Sabbath today demands sacrifice. When did it not? But the cost is small for so rich a blessing. Containing those forces of holiness and harmony, of love and law, which — by transforming the home into a sanctuary, the father into a priest, and the family into a sanctified unit — have helped mold the noble institution of the Jewish home, the Sabbath sets aside a day from commercial warfare that our tattered lives might be joined together once a week. It is the most powerful force we possess to counteract the breakdown of the family which grows more and more widespread, as well as to provide an answer to the problem of leisure which weighs so heavily upon people's minds.

We have underestimated the American Jew. He is no longer running away from Judaism. The challenge of the total Sabbath as an answer to the problems of modern man may find a deep and enthusiastic response on the part of thousands of Jews who are genuinely seeking a way of Jewish living and thinking.

We have failed to approach the Sabbath in the only way it can be approached, by saying to ourselves: "I am a child of the covenant; this is the sign of the covenant; it is the source of blessings untold for me and my family; it is what is asked of me as a Jew; let me — together with my family and my fellow Jews — learn to keep it."

V

A Ladder of Observance

Too often books have been written for the modern Jew which explain the importance of some aspect of Judaism without telling the reader how he might carry it out in his life. But there are many today, especially young people, troubled by what they see about them and eager to establish new patterns for their lives, who are ready to move from the "why" to the "how." Having had no pattern of Jewish observance from their parents to follow, they want to know for themselves what they are to do. It is for that purpose that this chapter has been added. But how could it best be of help to the reader? The only certain failure would be to strictly insist that all attempts at observance are to no avail unless the entire Sabbath is kept here and now. Rosenzweig's word of caution to the modern Jew must be remembered — not "all" or "nothing," but to begin with "something." This has been the unique approach of Conservative Judaism. Appreciating the situation of the modern Jew as inquiring but uncommitted, it offers a program which requires neither complete and immediate compliance with the law, nor total capitulation to the temper of the times, but rather, in the words of Abraham Heschel, a "ladder of observance," which each Jew is encouraged to climb at his own pace. Some of us may be at the very bottom; others may be several rungs up. What is important is not where we stand on the ladder at the moment, but that we are willing to try to move up rung by rung.

Before presenting the ladder itself, several preliminary remarks about goals and methods are in order.

To Keep It Holy; Not to Work*

There are two fundamental elements in the Sabbath *mitzvah,* as stated in the fourth of the Ten Commandments: a "thou shalt" and a "thou shalt not." The "thou shalt" says: "Remember and guard the Sabbath day, to keep it holy." The "thou shalt not" says: "the seventh day is a Sabbath to the Lord; do not do any work on it." Both elements, the negative and positive, are essential to the fulfillment of the *mitzvah* of Sabbath.

The negative element — "do not work" — is essential because resting itself — pausing, desisting, withdrawing, etc. — is necessary for life to be human, free, and because it guarantees the availability of energy and time for the positive element — "remember to keep it holy." Every Jew is commanded to observe the Sabbath in both phases: negatively, by refraining from work on the Sabbath; and positively, by remembering and guarding the Sabbath as a holy day. But the word "work" and the word "holy" require elaboration.

What Is "Work"?

What is work *(melakhah)?* Drawing upon the age-old Jewish search to understand what the Torah means by "work," we may say that work includes basically the following:

1) Earning one's livelihood, and engaging in any busi-

---

* I am grateful to Rabbi Hershel Matt for the material on the next few pages, which he has kindly allowed me to use (with some modification).

ness or commercial transactions — including shopping.

2) Performing strenuous physical exertion and carry-
ing burdensome objects from one place to another.

3) Changing the world of things by kindling or ex-
tinguishing a flame; by repairing, improving, con-
structing, destroying, planting, cooking, sewing,
writing, tearing — in a word, by basically altering or
making anything.

4) Traveling from one's community or neighborhood.

5) Making preparations during the Sabbath for after
the Sabbath.

6) Engaging in any activity that constitutes drudgery.

7) Allowing onself to be preoccupied, distracted, or
anxious about any of the above — or to be angry,
hateful, grieved, or despairing about anything.

8) Otherwise defiling, profaning, or cheapening the
precious holiness of the Sabbath — by deed, word,
or thought.

What Is "Keeping the Sabbath Holy"?

What do we mean by "keeping the Sabbath holy"?
Again drawing upon the Tradition, we may say that to
keep the Sabbath holy *(kadosh)*, includes, in addition to
abstaining from work, basically the following:

1) Cleaning, arranging and adorning one's home, one's
wardrobe and one's person — and preparing special
meals — in advance of the Sabbath in honor of the
Sabbath.

2) Providing for the needy in advance of the Sabbath;
and inviting the stranger, the needy, the lonely and
the troubled to share in one's Sabbath.

3) Welcoming the Sabbath with the lighting of candles and *Kiddush,* and ushering it out with *Havdalah.*

4) Studying Torah, individually or in groups.

5) Eating festive meals, wearing special clothes, taking a leisurely walk, taking special Sabbath rest.

6) Increasing one's appreciation and enjoyment of the creations of the human spirit — such as literature and song.

7) Deepening the level of love and affection, of concern and care, of sharing and understanding among members of the household and among friends.

8) Turning to God by praying the evening, morning and afternoon services (with a congregation if possible, or else privately) and by reciting the Grace before and after meals — in thankfulness and wonderment at the blessings of creation and the gift of rest; in gratitude for redemption from enslavement; in examination of conscience and request for forgiveness; in sympathy for human suffering and deprivation, and in resolve to aid in their alleviation; in renewal of the covenant-bond with the people Israel; and in petition for an increase in inner resources for living.

Before Beginning

1) Perhaps you cannot picture yourself being able now, or later, or ever, to observe the Sabbath completely. (In the ultimate sense, perhaps no one ever does observe it completely.) Possibly your present situation — as regards your work, your family, your background, your outlook, your readiness — prevents you from making a great or sudden change

in your pattern of Sabbath observance. Perhaps the members of the family are in varying situations and will therefore find it best to begin at different points. The important thing is to make a start. Begin now.

2) Ask yourself: Which forms of work are there which up until now I *have engaged in* on the Sabbath but from which, from now on, I can *regularly abstain?* ("Regularly" may mean less regularly than "always" — but it must also mean more regularly than "sometimes.") How many: five? three? one?

3) Ask yourself: Which forms of "keeping holy" are there which up till now I *have neglected* on the Sabbath but which I *can* from now on *regularly observe?* (Again: if not "always," then at least more than "sometimes.")

4) Remind yourself that "a little is a lot, if done with the right intention of heart *(kavanah)*."

After a Start Has Been Made

1) Ask yourself: Am I seeking God's help to keep me from becoming discouraged because of my difficulties thus far?

2) Ask yourself: Can I do more in seeking to derive blessing from the Sabbath? Are there additional aspects, approaches, dimensions? Is there a deeper level of piety in which I can observe?

3) Ask yourself: Am I seeking God's help to keep me from becoming satisfied with my accomplishment thus far?

Based on the concepts of *kedushah* (holiness) and *melakhah* (work) described above, review your present pattern of Sabbath observance. You may find it helpful to draw up a specific list of things to be done or avoided before, during and at the conclusion of *Shabbat*. Each item may be considered in terms of: (1) Do we now do this?; (2) If not, could we?; (3) If so, how can we begin?; (4) What have we done thus far?

Afterword

Adam was created on the sixth day, after God had made the rivers, the woods, the animals and fish, so that he could live in eternal bliss in the choicest place on all the earth, the Garden of Eden, with all he might desire at his fingertips. But on the very same day he was made and in rebellion to the very first warning God gave him, Adam sinned. He was to have been put to death on the morrow, the Sabbath. According to an old legend, however, as this was about to happen, the Sabbath herself came forward to plead before the Almighty. How could the holy day of peace be so desecrated? God listened to the Sabbath, and, on her account, Adam was delivered from Gehinnom. Then was Adam filled with a knowledge of the blessing and holiness of the Sabbath and began to sing "a song for the Sabbath day" (Psalm 92).

Adam is every Jew. Through the ages the Sabbath has shielded him at least once a week from troubles he had brought upon himself or with which an unfriendly world had afflicted him.

We need that protection today. Fearsome are the forces of destruction which rage within ourselves, our families and our world, threatening our sanity if not our lives.

The Sabbath can become our fortress. Within her walls we can find security for our souls. Within the shelter of her wings we can learn how to conquer the weekday. For on the Sabbath we return to our true selves. And understanding who we are — the children of Abraham, Isaac and Jacob — enables us to perceive from whence we have come — Sinai — and whither we are going — to the end of time, when all man's conflicts, with himself, with his fellow and with nature, will be resolved, the time which will be only Sabbath.

Jacob dreamed of "a ladder fixed in the earth, whose head reached the heavens."

Said Rabbi Pinhas of Koretz:

"*A ladder fixed in the earth* — these are the six days of the week.

"*Whose head reaches the heavens* — that is the Sabbath."

Notes

1. Megillah 9a; Genesis Rabbah 10.

2. Abraham J. Heschel, *The Sabbath: Its Meaning for Modern Man* (New York: Farrar, Straus and Young, 1951), pp. 54-55.

3. Heschel, *op. cit.,* p. 31.

4. Cited in Nahum N. Glatzer, *Franz Rosenzweig* (Philadelphia: The Jewish Publication Society of America, 1953), p. 357.

5. Heschel, *op. cit.,* pp. 13, 16.

6. *Ibid.,* pp. 22-23.

7. Erich Fromm, *The Forgotten Language* (New York: Rinehart and Co., 1951), pp. 244-45.

8. Samuel Raphael Hirsch, "The Sabbath," *Judaism Eternal,* edited and translated by Israel Grunfeld (London: Soncino, 1956), pp. 36-38.

9. *Ibid.,* pp. 5-7.

10. *Ibid.,* pp. 22-23, 30-31.

11. Herman Wouk, *This Is My God* (New York: Doubleday, 1959), pp. 59-60.

12. Anne Chamberlain, "Israel On Rush" in *Vogue,* July 1969, p. 11.

13. Rabbi Yosef Haym of Bagdad, *Ben Ish Hayil,* Part 1, sermon 3; cited in A. Kariv, *Shabbat U'moed* (Tel Aviv: Dvir, 1966), p. 61.
   "During the week," said the Rabbi of Sokotchov, "the body is drawn in one direction, the soul in another, and there is no peace between them. But on the Sabbath the body submits to the soul and the struggle subsides. So the words of the Talmud can be understood: 'The Sabbath candles are meant to bring peace within the home' — that is, within man who is himself the home that houses body and soul" (Kariv, *op. cit.,* p. 49).

14. Heschel, *op. cit.,* p. 29.

15. Glatzer, *op. cit.*, p. 526. "The Sabbath is an elevation of all things to their source" (The Rabbi of Ger, quoted in Kariv, *op. cit.*, p. 48).

16. Glatzer, *op. cit.*, p. 315.

17. Franz Kobler, *Her Children Call Her Blessed* (New York: Stephen Daye Press, 1955), p. 5.

18. Heschel, *op. cit.*, pp. 29, 31-32, 28.

19. *Otiot d'Rabbi Akiba*, 9b.

20. Kariv, *op. cit.*, p. 46.

21. I Maccabees 2:29-38.

22. William Farmer, *Maccabees, Zealots and Josephus* (New York: Columbia University Press, 1956), p. 76.

23. *Antiquities* 14:4.2-3, quoted in Farmer, *op. cit.*, p. 76.

24. "We Go Forth All to Seek America" by Anzia Yezierska in *The Golden Land*, edited by Azriel Eisenberg (New York: Yoseloff, 1964), p. 286.

25. Glatzer, *op. cit.*, p. 284.

26. Kariv, *op. cit.*, p. 46, quoting Rabbi Noah of Lekhovitz.

Index

88

Index by Jerome H. Kanner, Ph.D., L.H.D.